Change

How to bring real change to your life:
The psychology and secrets of highly effective people

Philip Copitch. Ph.D.

YOU MUST BE THE CHANGE YOU WANT TO SEE IN THE WORLD.

MAHATMA GANDHI

Written and illustrated by Philip Copitch, Ph.D.
Printed in the United States of America.

HERE TO SERVE YOU:

Hutzpah Press titles are available in quantity discounts for promotions, premiums and fundraisers.

Our titles can be custom imprinted with your company name and information.

FOR FURTHER INFORMATION
PLEASE CONTACT:

HUTZPAH PRESS
PO BOX 400
IGO CA 96047-0400

Please contact:
Geri Copitch, Sr. Editor
Geri@CopitchInc.com

Dr. Phil's web site:
www.CopitchInc.com

DEDICATION

I have been blessed with the honor of helping families grow to be more creative and caring. Over the years, many have told me at the end of a family therapy session, "This is a lot to remember, you should write a book!"

So, I dedicate this book to the patients who asked, no, demanded, that I write it.

Special thanks goes to my bride of over 20 years—Geri, an amazing person who warms the hearts of all who know her, and the only one I know who can put up with me.

Thank you for encouraging my behavior.

Philip Copitch, Ph.D.
2008

Tell me, I forget.

Show me, I remember.

Involve me, I understand.

Table of Contents

3. UNDERSTANDING GOAL SETTING 81

4. UNDERSTAND HOW TO CONTROL TIME...... 97

5. UNDERSTAND HOW TO WORK YOUR PLAN 145

6. IN CONCLUSION: BE CREATIVE... GO DO WELL! 183

7. FORMS 186

TABLE OF FIGURES

INTRODUCTION

Simply put, this workbook is about you winning at the game of life. It is a step-by-step guide that shows you how to get your needs met.

The best way to get your needs met is to communicate your needs well. This workbook was developed to assist you in communicating well. In the pages that follow, you will learn the major stumbling blocks that keep people from becoming highly effective.

In the following paragraph you will most likely come across terms that are new to you. Don't be intimidated; the words that follow will be second nature to you by the end of this workbook.

If you studied highly effective people, you would learn that these individuals avoid Thought Mines and negative self-talk. They excel at positive self-talk and use emotional frameworks that lead to healthy interpersonal relationships. Highly effective people have learned to communicate clearly. They consistently "read" their environment correctly. They avoid emotional conflicts and bring out the best in the people they encounter. Highly effective people build on their skills and are able to accomplish amazing feats.

You too can learn to be a highly effective person. For this to happen, you will need a few particular skills. These skills are not hard to master, and they will serve you for a lifetime.

The five skills you will need:

1. Understand your self-talk and your self-esteem
2. Understand your emotional frameworks
3. Understand goal setting
4. Understand how to control time
5. Understand how to work your plan

I hope you have noticed that the above are all about you. All about _you_ getting _your_ needs met.

Chapter 1

Understand your self-talk and your self-esteem

"What do you mean, 'Ya feel a little hyper'?"

1. UNDERSTAND YOUR SELF-TALK AND YOUR SELF-ESTEEM

Self-talk is shrink speak for the stuff that goes on in our heads that only we can hear. It is that internal dialogue that we keep with ourselves. Most of us do not really think about how we talk to ourselves—it just happens. But, self-talk is really important to understand if you wish to win in the game of life.

Self-talk is powerful. It comes from inside you. It comes from your past. It is a CD playing a familiar tune. If the tune is negative, it is hurtful in a negative way. If the tune is positive, it is helpful in a positive way.

Unfortunately, we are hard-wired to remember the negative better than the positive. Our brain lays down stronger negative memories than positive ones. Most people find that they can remember the negative events, the painful ones of their youth, more clearly than their positive memories.

TALK SENSE TO A FOOL AND HE CALLS YOU FOOLISH.

Euripides

SELF-TALK CAN BE IMPLANTED

A lot of our self-talk is accidentally implanted. Often, self-talk is given to us by others that we feel are powerful in our lives. Mothers, fathers, spouses, teachers, friends, to name a few, give us information about ourselves that we lay down as powerful memories.

WHEN I WAS BORN I WAS SO SURPRISED I DIDN'T TALK FOR A YEAR AND A HALF.

Gracie Allen

SELF-TALK IS MORE BELIEVABLE

Self-talk is the interpretation of a situation rather than the situation itself. This interpretation influences our emotions, behaviors and even our physiology. Because self-talk comes from inside, it avoids most of the filters that we learn to use to evaluate our environment. We take the self-talk thought as a fact. Often self-talk is treated like a fact with emotional baggage. Sometimes we don't even see the baggage, we combine it with a fact, making it an even bigger unexamined fact.

YOU MUST CONTROL YOUR SELF-TALK TO CONTROL YOURSELF

Thoughts that emanate from within are often stimulated by some external event. This makes your self-talk very powerful. So, if for example, your parents have called you stupid for twenty years, I suspect that when you are feeling upset or nervous you call yourself "stupid."

HOW IS SELF-ESTEEM BUILT?

Let's start off by defining what we are talking about. Self-esteem goes by many names. Some call it self-worth, others self-confidence. The high brow academic set use words like, "the sense of self" or "ego identity." Shakespeare said it best, "A rose, is a rose, is a rose," or something like that. The reality is that we all know what high self-esteem or low self-esteem looks like, but it is hard to put it into words.

In a nutshell, self-esteem is the internal belief we hold about ourselves. What makes it hard to understand and put into words is that it is ever changing. We hold different internal beliefs about our abilities dependent on the situation.

For example, my five-year-old son informed me that he couldn't pick up a hat in the side yard because of spiders. He hadn't seen any spiders, but he was obviously uncomfortable. When he was reminded that he had touched spiders before, he said, "Yeah, but that spider was not hiding to get me!" Is this a self-esteem issue? In a way. If, at five, Joshua felt comfortable enough within himself to handle the fears that he pictured, I would not have had to pick up the hat. But, is it a self-esteem problem? It definitely is not. Josh was not saying to himself, "I'm not able to pick up the hat." He was saying, "I'm afraid of spiders hiding under the hat and attacking me." Often parents confuse low self-esteem with reasonable fear.

The internal belief we hold about ourselves is somewhat situational. You may feel comfortable talking to a small group, but petrified about presenting to thirty-four regional sales managers. When we talk about self-esteem, it is important to listen to our own self-talk. If we focus too much on our initial behavior we often miss the true picture.

So, when we talk about self-esteem, we are really talking about the internal balance of our beliefs of our self-worth.

When we are born we enter the world with a personal makeup. This personal makeup is usually called our temperament. You interact with your world through your temperament.

Newborns seem to be "pre-wired" to investigate their world. Part of their temperament is to investigate and eventually build relationships with their new world.

Infant research has shown that newborns have the ability to "interact" with their caregivers from the first moments of birth. Their eyes are developed enough to focus on their mother's face during the first breast feeding. Infants are able to smell and remember their caregivers.

An individual's temperament is influential in the formation of the feeling of self-worth. We take this sense of self with us throughout our life. For example, a sixty year old can truly say that they are the same, but still a different person than they were when they were six. Our feelings of self-worth are with us for a lifetime.

THE BIRD NEST

Recently my family and I watched a Discovery Channel program about birds from around the world. The narrator explained how different birds build their nests. Some birds simply moved around a patch of dirt and called it home. Other birds carried twigs and grasses up into a tree and intertwined them to make a nice basket. One swallow carried beak-full's of mud, making a substantial "clay" pot to call home. A hyper little fellow swiped spider webs and sewed the sides of leaves together making a sturdy green hammock. The birds did all this by instinct. Each of the different birds was pre-programmed with the innate ability to build their species-specific nest. This is impressive.

We all build our self-esteem in a similar fashion. We pick and choose from our environment to form our belief of who we are. Our temperament tends to initiate the direction of what we notice. Then, as time goes by, our temperament is intertwined with

REST SATISFIED WITH DOING WELL, AND LEAVE OTHERS TO TALK OF YOU AS THEY PLEASE.

Pythagoras

ASSOCIATE YOURSELF WITH MEN OF GOOD QUALITY IF YOU ESTEEM YOUR OWN REPUTATION FOR 'TIS BETTER TO BE ALONE THAN IN BAD COMPANY.

George Washington

Philip Copitch, Ph.D.   11

our experiences to form the "self." Most researchers believe that the self is pretty much built by age two. Then, by age three, we start an internal dialogue with ourselves and we develop our opinion about whom we are...[1,2,3,4] This is the onset of self-esteem.[5]

THREE BASIC LEVELS OF SELF-ESTEEM

AN UNDERSTANDING HEART IS EVERYTHING IN A TEACHER, AND CANNOT BE ESTEEMED HIGHLY ENOUGH. ONE LOOKS BACK WITH APPRECIATION TO THE BRILLIANT TEACHERS, BUT WITH GRATITUDE TO THOSE WHO TOUCHED OUR HUMAN FEELING. THE CURRICULUM IS SO MUCH NECESSARY RAW MATERIAL, BUT WARMTH IS THE VITAL ELEMENT FOR THE GROWING PLANT AND FOR THE SOUL OF THE CHILD.

Carl Jung

Most people think of self-esteem as either high or low. It is important to understand that self-esteem is a continuum.[6,7] No one really has a high self-esteem; rather they tend to possess mostly high feelings of self-worth and an understanding about their limitations. Similarly, individuals with low feelings of self-worth believe poorly about themselves in most situations, but are able to get by and outwardly function in their world. They perceive themselves through low esteem glasses, reaching medium esteem in a few limited areas of their life. Figure 1 illustrates the continuum of self-esteem.

There are three basic levels of self-esteem — high, medium and low.

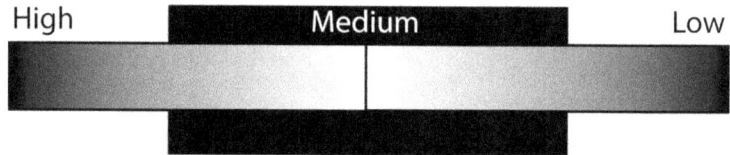

Figure 1: The Three basic levels of self-esteem

1- Winnicott, Donald W. (1960). Ego distortion in terms of true and false self. In The Maturational Processes and the Facilitating Environment. London: Hogarth and Institute for Psycho-Analysis, 1965.

2- Klein, Melanie. (1959). Our adult world and its roots in infancy. In Envy and Gratitude and Other Works 1946-1963. London: Hogarth, 1975.

3- Piaget, J. (1954). "The construction of reality in the child". New York: Basic Books.

4- Wadsworth, Barry J. Piaget's Theory of Cognitive and Affective Development: Foundations of Constructivism, 5th ed. Upper Saddle River, NJ: Allyn & Bacon, 2003.

5- Mruk, C. (2006). Self-Esteem research, theory, and practice: Toward a positive psychology of self-esteem (3rd ed.). New York: Springer.

6- Branden, N. (1969). The psychology of self-esteem. New York: Bantam.

7- Mecca, Andrew M., et al., (1989). The Social Importance of Self-esteem. University of California Press, 1989.

HIGH SELF-ESTEEM

A person with high self-esteem feels comfortable in most situations. She tests her beliefs and has had experience trusting her belief system. She is self-confident. She is aware that she thinks well on her feet. She knows that even well developed plans often need minor corrections. She is internally assured that she can deal with life's ups and downs. She is aware that she does not have all the answers while, at the same time knowing, deep in her soul, that she can figure out most of the answers she will need.

AN EXAMPLE OF HIGH SELF-ESTEEM:

Ellen is twelve years old. She is a hard working student who is somewhat bored in school. She is happy most of the time. Her parents are sure that she is a "good kid" who tends to be argumentative with them. "She is always testing my limits," her mother told me. "But then again, she plans to rule the world." Ellen feels good about herself and safe within her relationship with her parents. She has goals and dreams. She practices her growing skills on her parents. She chooses to back down when her parents give her firm limits.

MEDIUM SELF-ESTEEM

People with medium self-esteem are constantly questioning themselves. They know that they have done well, but are never really sure if it was their doing, or maybe just simple dumb luck. These people tend to have a hollow drive. It is not so much a quest for challenge, as in the high self-esteemer, it is a never-ending test of themselves, to see if they can cut the mustard. This need to prove themselves tends to be very taxing, removing much of the potential enjoyment from even doing well. Individuals with medium self-esteem are constantly in self-doubt.

AN EXAMPLE OF MEDIUM SELF-ESTEEM:

Summer is an outgoing, happy go lucky twenty-six year old. She has worked at the same office for three years. She doesn't really like her job, but she never seems to get organized enough to look for a better one. She would like to go to college, but has been unable to sign up at the junior college down the street. She seems to want help constantly. She needs others to direct her. She tends not to follow these directions, preferring to muddle her way through. She puts a lot of energy into almost getting things done, into almost taking control of her world.

LOW SELF-ESTEEM

People with low self-esteem are positive that they are doomed. They believe that any thought they have will prove to be stupid. Self-hate is the reality of people with low self-esteem. Self-hate leads to the use of societal anesthesia. This anesthesia tends to take the form of one or more of the following: social isolation, alcohol abuse, drug abuse, sexual promiscuity, or severe risk taking. Their mantra is "I don't care." And it is true for them. This internal pain drives them to wish out of a relationship, even with themselves. They often mistreat caring individuals in their world. They take the attitude, "If you care for me, you deserve whatever I do to you."

People with low self-esteem have no respect for themselves and only contempt for anyone who cares about them.

THE SUREST WAY TO CORRUPT A YOUTH IS TO INSTRUCT HIM TO HOLD IN HIGHER ESTEEM THOSE WHO THINK ALIKE THAN THOSE WHO THINK DIFFERENTLY.

Friedrich Nietzsche

TWO EXAMPLES OF LOW SELF-ESTEEM:

Dougie was a chubby man of thirty-six, married eighteen years, with three teenaged children. He came to see me because his wife was having her fourth affair. "Every now and then she just gets mean. She stops taking care of the kids and starts going out drinking. She doesn't even hide it any more."

Dougie has worked the same union job since high school. When I asked him about his chances of advancement he said, "Why bother to apply, they won't give me the job." Dougie was polite and talkative. He spoke of his dreams and goals. It was quickly apparent that he was positive, at the core of his being, that he would never come close to any of his dreams.

Arty was a muscular tattooed man of fifty. I was asked by his attorney to meet with him. For almost two hours he regaled me with stories of drinking, fighting and cheating on his two wives. He had a forty year history of doing what he wanted and not caring about anyone but himself. He had spent a total of 15 years in prison. He had held hundreds of menial jobs that he either quit, or got fired from. Anyone who cared for him he eventually alienated.

When I asked him what he thought about his life,

he looked at me and said softy, "It don't matter: I was born to die." I could feel his despair. All of his stories could not cover his self-loathing.

NOW FOR THE GOOD NEWS... SELF-ESTEEM IS NOT CARVED IN STONE

It is important that we seek the best building material available for growing our own self-esteem. Just as the bird forages for twigs, grasses, or mud, we search our environment for the stuff of self-esteem. At first, our information gathering process occurs mostly with our parents. In time, we become solely responsible for availing ourselves of safe, self-esteem nurturing, environments.

Research has shown us that newborns "pick up" on the feelings in their home.[8,9,10] We know that children who are physically cared for, but whose home is in emotional turmoil, tend to be prone to stomach unrest, headaches, and sleep disturbances.

Mrs. Rodriguez was going through a messy divorce with her abusive husband. Her family doctor saw her six-month-old daughter three times in one week for diarrhea and concerns of dehydration. Mrs. Rodriguez told me, "The doctor said all the tests came back normal. My baby was just fine. Then he whispered to me, 'Mary, I'm just a country doctor, but how about you send the baby to your mother's. Maybe she is all tied up in knots because of the family problems.' I told him that my husband and I don't argue in front of the baby, but I sent Alexa to my mother's anyway. You know, it was a miracle; she slept on the couch for the first fourteen hours. She got as big as a horse in just a week."

I think there is a lot to be said for country doctoring. Babies and young children are so dependent on their caregivers that it makes sense to me that they are critically attuned to them and their emotional states.

IT IS MUCH HARDER TO JUDGE YOURSELF THAN TO JUDGE OTHERS. IF YOU SUCCEED IN JUDGING YOURSELF, IT'S BECAUSE YOU'RE TRULY A WISE MAN.

Antoine de Saint-Exupéry
The Little Prince

NEVER ESTEEM ANYTHING AS OF ADVANTAGE TO YOU THAT WILL MAKE YOU BREAK YOUR WORD OR LOSE YOUR SELF-RESPECT.

Marcus Aurelius Antoninus

8- Carlson, Elizabeth A.; Alan Sroufe, L.; Egeland, Byron, The Construction of Experience: A Longitudinal Study of Representation and Behavior. Child Development, v75 n1 p66-83 Jan 2004.
9- Carlson, Elizabeth A.; Sroufe, L. Alan; Collins, W. Andres Early Environmental Support and Elementary School Adjustment as Predictors of School Adjustment in Middle Adolescence. Journal of Adolescent Research, v14 n1 p72-94 Jan 1999.
10- Ward, Mary J.; Carlson, Elizabeth A. Associations among Adult Attachment Presentations, Maternal Sensitivity, and Infant-Mother Attachment in a Sample of Adolescent Mothers. Child Development, v66 n1 p69-79 Feb 1995.

I once asked a young man, who just got an acceptance letter to college, how his mother reacted to the good news. He said, "She is very happy. But, she always told me I was special." "Special?" I questioned. "Yeah, she always told me I was special, you know, that I could put my mind to something and figure it out." "When did she tell you that you were special?" I continued. "Boy, knowing my mom, she probably patted herself on her belly and said, 'Whoever you are ... you're special to me." He smiled a big proud smile and I knew he was special. Why? Because I believed his mother.

HOW DO YOU BUILD YOUR OWN SELF-ESTEEM?

The simple answer is you control your environment. No matter where you are on the self-esteem continuum, low, medium or high, you build your self-steam by controlling the situations around you.

Who do you spend most of your time with? Are they good for you? Do you feed yourself a consistent diet of healthful thought? Do you read good uplifting books? Do you listen to uplifting music? Do you treat others well? Are you kind? Are you respectful?

What materials are in your world for you to build your self-esteem with? You have choices, are you making them? Who are you letting influence you?

Over the years, many amazing individuals have influenced me in a positive way. As an example, let me tell you about one such person, Dr. Jeffrey Smith. I was fortunate to take a course in graduate school from Jeffrey Smith, a celebrated psychologist and long time professor at Stanford University. When I showed up to my first class I had no idea who the instructor was. He arrived a few minutes before class was scheduled to begin and very slowly walked to a chair at the front of the room. He sat slowly. He spoke softly. He explained that he was an old man. He had a terminal disease and he hoped to be alive long enough to teach this 18 week course. He apologized for his frailty. He explained that he would understand if anyone would like to transfer to another instructor. He spoke about looking forward to meeting all of us young people. (Most were in their thirties.)

Dr. Smith captivated the class. It was obvious

A MIND, LIKE A HOME, IS FURNISHED BY ITS OWNER, SO IF ONE'S LIFE IS COLD AND BARE HE CAN BLAME NONE BUT HIMSELF.

Louis L'Amour
Bendigo Shafter

IF YOU WANT TO BE RESPECTED BY OTHERS THE GREAT THING IS TO RESPECT YOURSELF. ONLY BY THAT, ONLY BY SELF-RESPECT WILL YOU COMPEL OTHERS TO RESPECT YOU.

Fyodor Dostoevsky

to us that he wanted to die as he lived, a teacher. He let us know that we were special to him, that his world had greater meaning because we were a part of it.

Dr. Smith allowed us to experience his love. Soon after the course ended, Dr. Smith died. His wife mailed us our final exams. Until the end, Dr. Smith taught. He took the time to write a note on each final exam. My note was hard to read. The hand that penned it was weak. He wrote, "I like to think of you, by contrast, with your strong, positive spirit, working with children, Jeffrey"

I tucked Dr. Smith's belief in me into to my self-esteem nest. I have often thought about how honored I felt being in his class, and when I teach, I wish to emulate Dr. Smith's love and respect for his students.

THE MAN WHO BACKBITES AN ABSENT FRIEND, NAY, WHO DOES NOT STAND UP FOR HIM WHEN ANOTHER BLAMES HIM, THE MAN WHO ANGLES FOR BURSTS OF LAUGHTER AND FOR THE REPUTE OF A WIT, WHO CAN INVENT WHAT HE NEVER SAW, WHO CANNOT KEEP A SECRET - THAT MAN IS BLACK AT HEART: MARK AND AVOID HIM.

Cicero

THE BEST YEARS OF YOUR LIFE ARE THE ONES IN WHICH YOU DECIDE YOUR PROBLEMS ARE YOUR OWN. YOU DON'T BLAME THEM ON YOUR MOTHER, THE ECOLOGY, OR THE PRESIDENT. YOU REALIZE THAT YOU CONTROL YOUR OWN DESTINY.

Albert Ellis

NO ONE WANTS ADVICE, ONLY COLLABORATION.

John Steinbeck

Chapter Two

Viewing Your World With
Effective Emotional Frameworks

"Pregnant! But, what happens in Vegas stays in Vegas!"

2. VIEWING YOUR WORLD WITH EFFECTIVE EMOTIONAL FRAMEWORKS

Situations do not have feelings. We add the feelings to situations as they unfold before us. What I will be discussing here is your perceptions of your life. Your interpretation of what you think and do is your emotional framework. In this chapter we will dissect how we formulate and understand our world. First, we will look at personal responsibility. Then, we'll move on to how we can often misread a situation, and finally, end this chapter by looking at how we can control our perceptions.

YOU ARE 100% RESPONSIBLE FOR DEALING WITH YOUR LIFE

Over the years, my belief that we are all 100% responsible for our behaviors has produced predictable arguments from the adults I work with. On the surface, people are comfortable with this rule, as long as they read 100% as 93% or 97%. So let me make this clear, you are 100% responsible for how you deal with your life.

Mr. Griffith was a thirty-two year old father of three. He was arrested on December 24, for fighting in a hotel bar. When I talked with him in the jail's interview room he looked as if he lost the fight. He held ice to his swollen face and complained of loose teeth.

Mr. Griffith: It's not fair! I'm told that I have to stay in this $#%&^ place until after Christmas.

Dr. Phil: Sounds unpleasant, but how come you asked to see a therapist?

Mr. Griffith: I want you to tell them that they are #$%$^ing with my kids. It's not fair to my kids that they can't be with their dad on Christmas.

The point that Mr. Griffith didn't enjoy hearing was that he was blaming "them" for ruining his children's Christmas. The reality was that he was 100% responsible for getting arrested, and his be-

ONLY IN QUIET WATERS DO THINGS MIRROR THEMSELVES UNDISTORTED. ONLY IN A QUIET MIND IS ADEQUATE PERCEPTION OF THE WORLD.

Hans Margolius

Philip Copitch, Ph.D.   19

haviors lead to him not being available to spend Christmas with his children.

Taking 100% responsibility for dealing with your life is hard. It is multifaceted. Often it is a pain in the neck. It would be much easier if you just got to blame others.

The *American Heritage Dictionary* defines responsibility as:

> Involving personal accountability or ability to act without guidance or superior authority. Able to make moral or rational decisions on one's own, and therefore answerable for one's behavior.

So, if you don't get the promotion you desire, you are 100% responsible for how you deal with it. If your spouse walks out on you, you are 100% responsible for how you deal with it. If your children are hard to live with, you are 100% responsible for how you deal with it. If your car gets stolen, you are 100% responsible for how you deal with it.

At this point some smart individual likes to throw me a zinger. "You mean if a girl gets raped, or my mother gets shot by a gang banger, they're responsible?"

I say yes! You are always 100% responsible for how you deal with it. Read on...

RESPONSIBILITY DOES NOT MEAN BLAME

Responsibility is a person's accountability. My friend, Sally, who I have known since high school, called all in a dither. "Phil you have to help me … I have to lose 28 pounds by next Saturday!"

"What?" I questioned.

"I have to lose 28 pounds by next Saturday!" She whined. "I have to. My college reunion is next Saturday."

"Sally you can't lose that much by next Saturday." I said.

"I know, I know. But it's not fair. I've got to lose this baby weight."

"Baby weight, are you…?"

"Of course not, it's all Michael's fault."

"What? Michael, your Michael?" I asked.

"Yeah, it's all his fault, I put on this weight with him." She snarled.

"That makes no sense, Michael's 28, how can you blame him?" I asked.

"It's all his fault… that was a hard pregnancy."

Sally did not want to take any responsibility for her problem.

Let's look at this in a more serious situation. Stephanie was molested when she was six years old. She didn't tell anyone because her uncle was the molester. She was very confused and blamed herself for many years. She came to my office when she was twenty-four years of age. She had recently told the man she loved that she could not marry him. But, she could not tell him the reason why. Stephanie was afraid to have sex. This was not a huge problem while she was dating. Both of them were saving themselves for marriage. But she knew that she could not go on a honeymoon. You can't save yourself for marriage after you say "I do." At that point you have to "do." It took a lot of courage for Stephanie to reach out for help.

PAIN IS INEVITABLE; SUFFERING IS OPTIONAL.

Over the course of a year, Stephanie worked very hard in therapy to combat her fears. During our last session, I asked her to sum up her therapy experience.

> I learned that my uncle was to blame for betraying my trust in him, and that I was not responsible for being a victim at the age of six. But, I am responsible now if I feel like a six year old victim at the age of twenty-five.

After a long pause she continued.

> I also know that if I let my life get ruined because of my past that would be my fault. I am 100% responsible for how I deal with my life! I want a family. I deserve a family. And, I'm looking forward to getting pregnant.

We both cried with joy because we both knew that she was a powerful woman who understood personal responsibility.

YOU ARE 100% RESPONSIBLE FOR DEALING WITH HOW OTHERS TREAT YOU

Most people assume that they have little, if any, control over how others treat them. I believe the opposite to be true. I believe that you are 100% responsible for dealing with how others treat you. That doesn't mean that you have 100% control of how others act. It simply means that you are responsible for how you deal with how they act towards you.

Recently, a friend and I went out for our normal late Tuesday night dinner. Usually, the restaurant is almost empty. This particular night, the place was a mad house. It was packed with fire fighters just off the fire lines thirty miles away. The two waitresses were running all over, frantically trying to get the loud, hungry mass fed.

The bus boy noticed us and said he would clean a table for us in a few minutes. My friend and I sat reading the menu. He said, "We're never getting served today!"

"It'll be OK," I said.

When the waitress made her way to our table she looked like she had been put through a blender. Her hair was a mess, her little purple decorative apron was stained, and she seemed all jittery.

"Wow, you seem to be really overworked tonight. Are you OK?" I inquired.

"Hungry ... rude ... fire fighters," She gasped. "They all want steak at the same time." She wiped her brow with her forearm.

She told us that since four o'clock the place had been packed with hungry fire fighters. The kitchen was not set up for cooking this many steaks at one time, and two waitresses were not enough.

"It sounds unfair how you're being treated. When you have a minute for me let me know." I said.

"No, it's OK. What do you want? I'll get it for you. I don't care if they starve!" She said with a smile.

We were taken care of very well. The reason was because I treated the waitress with respect and empathy. I let her feel like a nice person, and she subsequently acted towards me like a nice person. I'm sure that she was choosing to treat my table nicely, because she surely had no trouble growling at the loud table in the far corner.

No man has the right to dictate what other men should perceive, create or produce, but all should be encouraged to reveal themselves, their perceptions and emotions, and to build confidence in the creative spirit.

Ansel Adams

As you go through your world you need to take responsibility for getting your needs met. If I were grumpy with the overworked waitress she would have seen me as one of the loud mass of humanity that filled her restaurant. But, recognizing that she was being put upon by her situation let her see me as a nice guy she wanted to feed. We both won. She felt appreciated and I got fed.

WHAT DO YOU PRESENT TO THE WORLD?

I told the story above to a sixteen-year-old boy who had been referred to my office because of his argumentative nature in school.

Benjamin: It's not fair. If I go into a restaurant and the waitress is having a bad day, she has no right to treat me like $#!*. She works for me, doesn't she?

Dr. Phil: I guess she works for you, but she is a person, isn't she?

Benjamin: So ... she's a person with a job. I shouldn't have to kiss her ass just for her to do her job.

Dr. Phil: Is that what I was doing, kissing ass?

Benjamin: Most definitely. 'You're working hard.' 'You're being mistreated!' He mimicked. She shouldn't take a job she didn't want. She is getting paid to get food for people and not to bitch.

Dr. Phil: I'll give you that what you are saying is true. But, none of that really matters to me. I wasn't nice to her because I had to be nice to her. I was nice to her because I wanted to be. In fact, I wanted to be served food in a timely manner. And, I didn't want her to growl at me. I was getting my needs met. It was also nice for the waitress, but that wasn't the reason I went to the restaurant, to be nice to a waitress. I went to the restaurant to get dinner. The way I interacted with the waitress got my needs met.

Benjamin: Oh, that's great for you with all your psychology. But I run into people that dump on me all the time.

Dr. Phil: Like at school?

Benjamin: Right. My first period teacher is a bitch to everyone. She doesn't care if I'm tired or if I have a headache. She just is on me, "Where's your homework," "Don't talk to me with that attitude!" I hate her and she knows it. So she takes any opportunity to jump on my back.

Dr. Phil: You mean if you turned in your homework, and were talking to her politely, she'd complain?

Benjamin: No. Of course not. She would probably find someone else to bitch at.

Dr. Phil: So, you're saying you're involved with her bitching at you?

Benjamin: I didn't say that, she just hates me.

Dr. Phil: It sounds to me that she will find someone else to hate if you don't fuel her fire by not turning in your homework.

Benjamin: Yeah, I guess. But, she works for me and she just bitches at me.

Dr. Phil: Let me understand this. Your teacher works for you? Her job is to get you to learn stuff? She thinks that you doing your homework will help you learn? It sounds like you have a pretty good employee for first period.

Benjamin: (with a smile) I hate when you make this all my stuff.

It was Benjamin's job to learn. Instead of taking that responsibility on his own shoulders, it was easier for him to blame his teacher. In fact, it was easier for him to blame his mother, his ex-girlfriend, and his grandparents for the problems in his life. He was the king of blaming others for his crappy relationships. It wasn't until he started to take personal responsibility for how he treated others and how others treated him, that his life became rewarding.

It is not until you accept 100% responsibility for dealing with your life that you will start to have a positive influence on how you treat others and others treat you.

Emotional frames are the borders that we see our world in. Imagine taking a full sheet of paper and cutting a small square in the center of it. The paper would become a frame for the small square you removed. If you put the paper in front of your face, and peered through the small opening, the paper frame would limit your view. You would still see a lot, but your view would be significantly limited. The paper frame would become your visual filter.

If you wore the frame in front of your face, over time your limited view would become normal to you. In fact, if you wore the paper frame from birth, you would not know what you did not know.

If this frame were filtering your emotions, rather than your sight, you would probably misinterpret interpersonal communications on a regular basis. And you probably wouldn't even know that you were misinterpreting.

This emotional framework and emotional filtering is very important. It is part of who we are every second of our life. It is how we view and feel about our life experiences. Let me give you a simple example:

I needed to pop into the hardware store to replace my old wrench. It wasn't the most important thing in the world to do, but I wanted to do it. When I got to the store, the parking lot was packed. Later, I found out that there was a big pre-pre Christmas sale. I parked at the farthest parking lot, in the last row. I was barely in the same county as the store.

At this point, I began to *think about my thinking*. At the simplest level I had two thoughts.

1. "What a pain in the neck. I have to walk all the way over there just for the privilege of buying a wrench."
2. "What a nice opportunity. I get a nice brisk walk and get to go buy a wrench."

WISE MEN TALK BECAUSE THEY HAVE SOMETHING TO SAY; FOOLS, BECAUSE THEY HAVE TO SAY SOMETHING.

Plato

THOUGH I AM NOT NATURALLY HONEST, I AM SO SOMETIMES BY CHANCE.

William Shakespeare

These two emotional frameworks seem pretty similar. But they most definitely are not. The first emotional framework defines my world as inconvenient. It makes me the victim of a mass conspiracy of mega corporate hardware stores who forced me to suffer a several-minute walk.

The second emotional framework allows me to experience the blessing of a healthy four-minute walk to do what I want.

We all have a running dialogue narrating our life (self-talk). If the dialogue is negative once a day, no big deal. But, if the dialogue is constantly negative, hour after hour, day after day, we become negative. You are, or will become, what you think about the most. If you have millions of negative thoughts you will become a person weighed down by negative thoughts.

On the other hand, if you have millions of positive thoughts, you will become a person who is uplifted by millions of positive thoughts.

Please think about this at a very selfish level. If you could choose positive over negative, why would you chose negative? Which would be better for you? By being aware of your self-talk, and your emotional frameworks you can uplift yourself. Who better to help you, than you?

UNDERSTANDING THOUGHT MINES

Thought Mines are social misreadings that get in the way of communicating clearly. They are thought stumbling blocks that allow us to misread, and often misjudge, the intention of others. By misreading others intentions, we can often get sidetracked from getting our needs met.

There are sixteen Thought Mines listed below. Each Thought Mine is followed by a definition and several examples. The example categories are:

· Negative self-talk example
· Couple example
· Teen example
· Work/school example

The examples are typical sentences that illustrate that particular Thought Mine. Negative self-talk is a thought, whereas the categories: couple, teen, or work/school, are representative sentences. These examples are not set in stone. It is common for a Thought Mine to be in more than one category at the same time. The important thing is that you notice it as a Thought Mine. The act of noticing the Thought Mine allows you to control it. We all have Thought Mines. If you do not control them, they will control you.

The order of the following Thought Mines is based on what I see in my office, ranked from most common to least common. Most Thought Mines occur without warning. As the stress in one's life increases, the intensity and frequency of the Thought Mines increase, often to the point where the mere presence of the other person, or the situation, is revolting and painful. Please note, a situation (or a person) simply is. We interpret it as a positive or a negative. This will be discusses in more detail later in the section, Control your perceptions.

Each Thought Mine is followed by a definition and a list of examples. Please note that the following examples are representative statements. The same sentence may represent numerous Thought Mines. I list examples mainly to give you a starting point. Often individuals blend two or three "favorite" Thought Mines together into their own type of social misreading.

THOUGHT MINE #1: HYPERBOLE

Definition:	Exaggerating to prove a point to yourself or others. Deliberate and obvious exaggeration used for effect.
Negative self-talk example:	· "It always happens to me… I can never get a break." · "The doctor said it was the worst wrist break he had ever seen."
Couple example:	· "He is the most insensitive and hateful person on the planet." · "She is the weirdest person I have ever met."
Teen example:	· "You always think the worst of me!" · "I wish I had never been born!"
Work/ school ex:	· "Thompson is the worst teacher I have ever had. He hates me and I know it!"

Using hyperbole (hy·per·bo·le), to hyperbolize, is a normal part of expression. When Dad walks into the kitchen and exclaims, "I could eat a horse!" We wouldn't expect Mom to growl back. "Well, unfortunately for you, we only have spaghetti. No matter what I make you complain!" However, a couple told me this exact story as proof that their marriage was over.

Usually, hyperbole is a communication tool. It is a way to emphasize a point. But, when a person feels emotionally raw, hyperbole is a ticking bomb.

Comedians use hyperbole to shock laughter out of an audience. "My wife is so frigid, that when she opens her mouth a little light comes on." That's a funny line unless a couple is having problems in the bedroom and the husband tells this joke at a party. This hyperbolic joke could be interpreted as an emotional knife in her heart.

Many Thought Mines are hyperbolic. The intent of the statement or the interpretation by the listener, is what causes heartache. Hyperbole is a window into one's feelings. By understanding the underlying feeling, you can learn to communicate more clearly.

Often, hyperbole within a troubled relationship (work or home) is seen as a character attack. "I work hard all day, is it too much to ask that you keep the damn kids quiet during dinner!" This type of statement is layered with hyperbole and implied wrongdoing. The kids are bad, the spouse is a bad mother, the husband does the most work and the wife's work is not as important. Or, it could simply mean that Dad has a headache and needs a quiet room.

Other times, hyperbole within a troubled relationship is seen as a plea for pity. "My back was killing me while I was doing the dishes."

This often is perceived as weakness and leads to a verbal attack by the other. These attacks are often focused on one word. "You're saying I NEVER do the dishes! How dare you act as if you do EVERYTHING around here!"

These types of continual emotional Thought Mines often emotionally drain normally caring people.

THOUGHT MINE #2: IRRATIONAL LABELING

Also called:	Negative labeling, Labeling is disabling
Definition:	Using a label to define a person, place, situation, or yourself.
Negative self-talk example:	• "I'm such a dummy!" • "I must be cursed… this keeps happening to me." • "Why would she go out with me, I'm fat."

Couple example:	• "She is just like her mother." • "He is a control freak." • "She is so paranoid, she is driving me crazy." • During a long car ride: "She is not talking to me, she must be mad at me again."
Teen example:	• "The teacher is a bitch!" • "I saw you talking to him, you're such a slut." • "Everyone thinks that they're my boss!" • While sitting down to dinner, thinking to yourself: "I'm tired of chicken, Mom must be mad at me again."
Work/ school ex:	• "My supervisor is just hanging on 'till retirement, he's simply useless." • "Betty's such a brown nose…"

Using a label tends to mean you have run out of words. When people run out of words they tend to show frustration.

Three-year-olds bite or tantrum when they run out of words to express their feelings. School age children tend to swear and hit when they run out of words. Adults tend to swear and irrationally label when they run out of words.

Abigail was a thirty-two year old mother of three. She was in my office because her oldest son was getting into trouble at school. To say the least, she was frustrated with her life.

Abigail: My husband is a complete moron when it comes to the children. He loves them, don't get me wrong. But he doesn't care about their education.

Dr. Phil: Excuse me for asking, but … does your husband have a learning disability?

Abigail: No, no, no—he's really smart. He just acts like a moron around the kids.

Dr. Phil: I don't understand, what do you mean by "moron."

Abigail: You know what I mean. He won't listen to me. No matter what I say, he won't do it.

What Abigail was stating, with her irrational labeling, was that her husband disagreed with her. By using the word "moron" she didn't have to deal with the fact that a person she thought intelligent disagreed with her. Once the irrational labeling was brought to her awareness, Abigail and her husband proved to be a formidable team to motivate change in their son's school behavior.

THOUGHT MINE #3: BLACK AND WHITE THINKING

Also called:	All or nothing thinking. Polarized thinking. Light switch thinking (on/off)
Definition:	Viewing a person or situation as having only two choices such as: good/bad, positive/negative, smart/dumb, happily married/divorced
Negative self-talk example:	• "People are pretty or ugly, I'm not pretty, so I must be ugly."
Couple example:	• She: "You haven't touched me in a week, are you having an affair?" • He: "You haven't let me touch you in a week…do you hate me?"
Teen example:	• "I'm still a virgin, I'll never get laid."
Work/school ex:	• "I don't have a job. Who would want to hire me? Only losers don't have a job." • "I'm not happy here, I should just quit."

Black and White Thinking is very common even among happy couples, motivated coworkers, and close friends. In such situations the black and white thinking causes short term distress, which will naturally dissipate over a small amount of time. However, when stress increases the tension in the relationship, black and white thinking leads to limited options (only 2) that dictate how a person feels about the other, and how one acts towards the other.

One couple of 28 years that I worked with became stuck at two choices. The wife put it this way, "Either I do whatever he says, pretending that I have no thoughts, or we get divorced." When the couple understood that their problem was not an on or off light switch, but a dimmer switch with millions of options, they worked diligently together looking for choices and options which would work best for them.

It is important to note, that for 28 years, black and white thinking had worked well for them. It wasn't until extreme stresses lead the couple to an all or nothing answer, which time could not dissipate, that they had a real family crisis.

As Beck[11] explains:

> Under stress, people's thinking about complex problems slide into familiar, pre-formed grooves. The "solutions" represented by these grooves are simplistic: give in or get out; fight or flight, shout or shut up.

Black and white thinking makes thinking all positive or all negative.

all bad — all good
all happy — all sad
all positive — all negative

Black and white with shades of gray:

Good · Calm · Bad

Free from agitation, excitement, or disturbance

Figure 2: Spectrum of black and white thinking

Calm is balanced and relaxed— conducive to thought.

A teenager asked me, "So, you're saying I should never be angry?" To this I pointed out that the problem was with the word *be*. One is not an angry, or a happy or a sad. These words are feelings not a state of being. You are a person who presently feels angry. That is different than being an angry person. Anger is a useful emotion, but I advise feeling calm while acting angry. Anger leads to escalation, while calm leads to self-control.

When feeling sad, strive for calm. Calm leads to thought and understanding.

When feeling bad, strive for calm. Calm leads to insight and self-respect.

Often individuals believe that they should be, or even that they have the right, to feel happy all the time. This is a time bomb. A healthy life is spent feeling calm, feeling in balance.

When people feel sad most say to themselves, "I want to feel happy" or "I deserve to feel happy." However, a healthy and emotionally honest question would be, "What do I need to do to get back to feeling calm?" This question puts you back in control of you. The thought, "What do I need to do?" puts the responsibility for how you act squarely on your shoulders. Who else should be re-

11- Beck, Aaron T. Love is Never Enough. HarperPerennial, 1988.

sponsible for how you act?

THOUGHT MINE #4: PRACTICED HOPELESSNESS

Also called:	Irrational hopelessness
Definition:	Believing that something cannot be done and avoiding any evidence that does not support your hopelessness.
Negative self-talk example:	• "There's no way I can do that, why bother?"
Couple example:	• "My mom never owned a house, we don't need to own our own home."
Teen example:	• "No one in my family has ever gone to college, why should I care about grades?" • "We're all going to die, so who cares about smoking?"
Work/ school ex:	• "I'd have to take a bus if I worked over there." • "I'm not good at math. Why should I bother looking into a G.E.D.?"

I want to tell you a story of an amazing woman who was frozen by practiced hopelessness. On the surface this sounds improbable. How can a person be "amazing" and also "hopeless" at the same time?

Easily. We humans compartmentalize. We can be amazing in one area, and perceive ourselves as totally incapable in another.

Amanda came to see me because she was "stressed at work." Amanda had built a law practice in fifteen years that was the envy of her friends and colleagues. In addition to her career, she was highly involved with two charities and her church.

After listening to Amanda for fifteen minutes I asked, "Why are you really here, you don't seem all that stressed to me."

"I don't know what to call it…" she said as she looked at her shoes, "I know I can't complain, but…"

After a long pause I said. "Amanda, just say what needs to be said, I can't help if I'm not trusted."

At this, Amanda sat straight upright, took a deep breath, and blurted out a speech that I suspect had been welling up inside for some time. "I need sex. I need a man! Not just a one night stand. I need a real man. I want a man who isn't afraid of me. I want children, vacations and passion."

"I take it that you're finding it hard to date?" I asked.

Before I share her answer with you, I want you to be ready. I want you to notice how hopeless Amanda explained her situation. How well practiced her belief was that her situation was "hopeless".

"Date? Who has time to date? And whom would I date? Either I have to dumb myself down for a knuckle dragging mouth breather, or I can hop into bed with a self-obsessed egotist who probably is married. Who would want me anyway? I can't cook and I work constantly. I can't see me in a mini van. And kids, I don't know the slightest thing about kids. I don't think it's right for a child to know their nanny better than their own mother."

Amanda laid out all of her fears and concerns. With this degree of internal conflict it was easy for her to feel hopeless. The more these thoughts ruminated, the more she practiced hopelessness.

Practiced hopelessness is a learned behavior. Anything that can be learned can be unlearned and replaced with a more functional behavior.

THOUGHT MINE #5: MAGNIFICATION (OFTEN RELATED TO CATASTROPHIZING)

Also called:	Exaggerating
Definition:	Exaggerating the importance of a person or situation. Using words like never, nothing, everything, or always.
Negative self-talk example:	• "If I don't get to see her today, she'll never go out with me."
Couple example:	• "You're spending is going to lose us everything we own."
Teen example:	• "You always yell at me."
Work/ school ex:	• "If I don't pass this test, I'll never get into college." • "I never get the credit for anything I do around here."

Often, magnification looks more like minimization. What this means is that in order to magnify the negative, one has to minimize the positives. One mom said, "Although my girls have all their grandparents, loss of the kindly old lady down the street will crush them."

Magnification tends to produce an emotional roller coaster that leads to turmoil and unnecessary sadness.

Mr. Roland entered my office in a rush. His face was flushed and he seemed to be fighting back tears. After working for the school district for fifteen years he applied for a similar job in a different department. The new job offered more advancement in the future.

Mr. Roland: I really failed this week. I am never going to get the promotion I deserve.

Dr. Phil: What happened?

Mr. Roland: (speaking quickly) Everything I have been working for went up in smoke. Just like that, gone! I'm a jerk for hoping, that's it. I'm just a jerk. My career is kind of over. I can't believe it. I royally screwed up. I don't know how I'm going to tell Mary (wife). I always screw up. I'll never be a department head; I can't even get a transfer position.

Dr. Phil: Take a breath and tell me what we are talking about.

Mr. Roland: (Somewhat calmer) I just found out that I didn't get the position I applied for. Everything I try is… you know. I just screw up everything.

It took Mr. Roland twenty minutes to calm his thoughts down. His use of words like "never", "always," and "everything" fueled his frustration. By using these words Mr. Roland was attacking his own character. This character attack was very painful and unnecessary.

After Mr. Roland was calm he was able to see that his world was safe and his future had lots of potential.

THOUGHT MINE #6: CATASTROPHIZING (OFTEN RELATED TO MAGNIFICATION)

Definition:	Expecting negative and exaggerated consequences. Expecting events to become terrible, disastrous, dreadful, appalling, horrific, shocking, or awful.
Negative self-talk example:	• "Christmas at Mom's house always leads to an argument."
Couple example:	• "If we drive home late we could die an awful death."
Teen example:	• "If I don't have those shoes I'll have no friends."
Work/ school ex:	• "My boss hates me and probably wants to fire me. It's just a matter of time."

A few weeks after Mr. Roland did not get the lateral job position he wanted, he told me about an argument with his wife, Mary.

Mr. Roland: Mary is trying to be supportive, I guess. She is constantly on me about applying for a new position. Constantly, and I mean constantly, she is hounding me to make a change. She just doesn't understand how hard it is to get a better job!

Dr. Phil: Are you interested in changing your job?

Mr. Roland: Sure, I want to. But, why bother. I'm going to get my hopes up and then… BLAM! I'll probably end up getting fired from the job I have.

Dr. Phil: Fired?

Mr. Roland: My boss will probably fire me because he will think that I'm not working hard enough. You know, he may get tired of dealing with me. Mary doesn't understand. We have been arguing all week. She never lets go of an argument. She's like a pit-bull, and I can't get her to understand that I don't want to lose my job.

Mr. Roland was still angry about not getting his desired job. Often magnification and catastrophizing become an angry dance. This dance was leading to arguments at the Roland house. (Note: Mr. Roland used the words "constantly" and "pit-bull" the same way he used the words "never", "always" and "everything" back in the section on magnification.)

Catastrophizing often hides anger. The angered individual perceives the catastrophe then uses that pent up anxiety to lash out at the other. The act of lashing out often relieves the attacker's anxiety—leaving the victim of the emotional attack the only one still angry. The attacker often falls back into magnification (i.e., "You never let go of an argument." or "You take everything too seriously, you always overreact."). This allows the cycle to start anew.

THOUGHT MINE #7: MIND READING

Also called:	Projection
Definition:	Irrational concern about what the other person thinks about you. Making negative assumptions about another's thoughts or motives. Assuming that others think or feel the same way you do. Especially about negative thoughts or impulses.

Negative self-talk example:	· "He thinks I'm talking too much."
Couple example:	· "You know that you only think of me as your sex toy!"
Teen example:	· "My parents hate me. They just have to say they love me because it's a law or something."
Work/ school ex:	· "They never ask me to go to lunch because they know I didn't go to college."

Often individuals who mind read see in others the negative thoughts, feelings, or impulses that they are personally fighting to control. An example of this would be a mother who constantly harps on her daughter about food choices when she herself harbors a desire to lose weight. Mind reading pushes people away.

It is usually best to deal with mind reading head on. Point out the fact that it is inappropriate to muck around in someone else's thoughts, and that it is impossible to do so. Worrying about another's thoughts is a personal distraction and a waste of energy.

It doesn't matter what people think … only what they do. Words count a little; actions count a lot. It is best to judge others by their actions. Time spent believing that you know what anyone is thinking is a waste of your time. A patient with AIDS told me, "I now understand that you never know someone else's sexual history, no matter what you may believe."

Spend your time focusing on clearly observing behaviors if you want to begin to know another person. (And assume you still know very little.) It is often simplest to ask about someone's thoughts. Most people love to talk about themselves, and what is more about them, than their thoughts.

THOUGHT MINE #8: FORTUNE TELLING

Also called:	Forecasting
Definition:	Negative predictions about your future. Predicting personal failures.
Negative self-talk example:	· "I blew that interview. Why bother going to the one this afternoon."
Couple example:	· "You know you're going to be late, so don't have a lame excuse this time."

Teen example:	· "No matter what I do, I can't get a good grade."
Work/ school ex:	· "I hate going to meetings, no one ever listens to my ideas."

This is the realm of personal self-esteem destruction. I like to say, "You are, or will become, what you think about the most." Prolific forecasters tend to emotionally spiral into depression.

Fortune telling gives one permission to fail. Simply put, if you know your future, and are sure that in this future you have failed, why bother? The problem with this idea is that the future is unwritten. And the future takes a circuitous path.

If you read the history of highly effective individuals, you will find that the path they took to being noteworthy was indirect. By pretending that you know the future, and that it is bleak, you force yourself to fail because you never try.

One sign of fortune telling is the use of the word "lucky" when describing someone else's great deed. "My brother Larry is so lucky. He has a big house and three cars." By using the word "lucky" this way you are leaving out the fact that Larry worked hard for twenty years to build his skills so he could land the job that lead to his fat pay check. This type of luck comes to hard working men and woman. In fact, the word deed means "intentional act."

THOUGHT MINE #9: FILTERING

Also called:	Mental filtering Selective abstraction Discounting
Definition:	Discounting information that does not fit your present argument.
Negative self-talk example:	· "Why try a new alarm clock, I always sleep through my alarm."
Couple example:	Sally: "I will never get married because I'm fat." Dr. Phil: "Do you know anyone who is as big as you who has gotten married?" Sally: "I have two friends who are bigger than I am who got married."

Teen example:	Teen: "In the last month I have only snuck onto the computer one time. One time!"
	Mom: "I understand that, but the one time was yesterday."
Work/ school ex:	• "I don't care about the nice things my boss wrote on my quarterly evaluation, I know he's planning on giving me a poor annual evaluation."
	• "I'm getting D's on my homework, but I'll do OK on the final, why start studying now?"

By filtering out information that is inconvenient to one's argument, an individual can easily find the answer that he or she wants to find.

A common joke heard in college statistics classes is, "Nine out of ten doctors think the tenth doctor is an idiot." By disregarding opposition to your thought it is easy to be misinformed.

Filtering is a form of lying; lying by avoiding important information. "What my wife doesn't know won't hurt her," is a common couple-filtering problem. This type of belief system tends to undermine a relationship, making it extremely weak over time.

By filtering communication one tends to avoid personal responsibility.

The best way to deal with filtering is to argue with yourself. Question your own authority. Ask yourself how you could do something differently. Become your own devil's advocate. This way you can provoke an internal discussion. Take the other side of the argument and find the strongest evidence for that stance. Challenge yourself.

Challenge others in the same way. (Via discussion, not argument.) I was once in a lively discussion with a colleague concerning the scientific proof of psychic phenomenon. After an hour of opinion and counter opinion I took my own advice. "Gust, in your expansive understanding of the literature, what is the best evidence that there is no such thing as psychic phenomenon?" After a long thought he said, "I am quite surprised that we have not one iota of evidence of interstellar psychic or future transverse psychic phenomena." Well, that tightened up my side of the debate. Even if I had no idea what it meant, the obvious gaping lack of interstellar and future transverse data seemed to be all the proof I needed. But seriously, it is important to look at all sides of an issue to help you get to the best answer. Purposefully leaving out information is a form of lying to yourself.

Definition:	Seeing only a small aspect of the whole situation, usually the biggest negative.
Negative self-talk example:	• "If she liked me she'd sleep with me."
Couple example:	• She: "I work too—you never let me buy jewelry." • He: "The rent is due in three days. And I work hard too, why can't I buy another dirt bike?"
Teen example:	• "I can't get into college, the counselor said that the 'schools are choosy.'"
Work/ school ex:	• At a meeting, the supervisor said, "Over the next three months there will be a few changes, mainly in the accounting paperwork. This should help us keep to the budget." Mary heard, "changes" to mean she was getting laid off.

Erma, at thirty-two, was a highly motivated gourmet chef working at a high-class restaurant. After seven years with the same owner, her world became intolerable when the restaurant was sold to an international corporation.

Erma: I don't think I can take it anymore. The new boss is a tyrant. He is watching everything I do. He micro manages. He is always hovering. He told me to watch my plate presentation. Me… I can't believe he is watching me. I know my way around the kitchen. You know he doesn't even cook! He just watches.

Dr. Phil: The new boss doesn't cook?

Erma: He doesn't lift a finger to help. He watches me all day. He is a corporate suit. He doesn't care about anything but making money.

Dr. Phil: How do you know.

Erma: I know!

Dr. Phil: How do you know?

Erma: I know because he said that he was there to make everything run smoothly. And all he does is watch me. As if I'm the problem. I can't take this any more.

Erma was upset for weeks about being watched by the new boss. Often, she would tell me wonderful improvements at work due to the change in ownership. She got better health insurance, longer paid vacation, and stock options, but she still focused on the "…suits watching me." Erma did not like working for a large corporation. She didn't like having suits in the kitchen. Eventually, she took a different position with lower pay and far less perks. Her new job was working for a small college as the resident chef. She told me that she liked the new job, but she missed the excitement of a first class kitchen and the camaraderie of foodies.

The part I left out of the story was, that according to Erma, the "suits" spent about 30 minutes a week in the kitchen, but in her thoughts they were there most of the time.

THOUGHT MINE #11: EMOTIONAL REASONING

Also called:	Gut reasoning Feelings as facts
Definition:	Knowing something is a fact because you feel it is a fact. Allowing your thoughts (and actions) to be unduly influenced by your feelings or present mood. Often evidence contrary to your feelings is disregarded.
Negative self-talk example:	· "What a headache, this will be a crappy day for sure!"
Couple example:	· "You know I'm tired, so why are you on my case now?" · "If you loved me, you'd know that you're bothering me!"
Teen example:	· "That'll be fun, let me have some of those pills."
Work/ school ex:	· "I just got in the door, why couldn't you kids just give me a minute to myself." · "I hate math, why do I have to take another math class!"

By using feelings as facts, one can give oneself permission to do almost anything. I once worked with an angry young man charged with murder. He stated, "If he (the victim) didn't want to die he shouldn't have come to the ATM." When I asked him to explain this he emoted, "He put himself in danger, if you put yourself in danger, you could die. When the lion kills the deer, he ain't being mean to the deer, is he?"

Unfortunately, emotional reasoning is pervasive in our society.

I feel this thought so it must be a correct thought.

A local businessman told me, "If Hillary Clinton gets into office we won't be able to afford employees." When I questioned his assumption, he said, "It just makes sense, Democrats love taxes, and Hillary is the worst type of Democrat, so it means even worse taxes." This is an illogical form of syllogism that should be left for late night television comedians. This businessman was allowing his dislike for a candidate to justify his business worries. This type of emotional reasoning could lead to humongous business and personal mistakes.

THOUGHT MINE #12: JUDGING

Also called:	Imperatives
Definition:	Having a fixed, critical view of self or others. Often using should have, should not have, ought to, must, mustn't, never, have to, could have, or you better, to make a statement rigid and seemingly factual.
Negative self-talk example:	· "If he loved me he would have called already."
Couple example:	· "You should have called me as soon as you knew." · "You ought to respect me, I'm your wife!"
Teen example:	· "If you don't like my attitude, you shouldn't have pissed me off." · "You better get off my back, or I'll …"
Work/ school ex:	· "You have to give me a "C", my parents will kill me if I get a "D" in this stupid class." · "You never think about how that affects me!"

As I tell my kids, the shouldas, the wouldas, and the couldas, are not famous tribes. They are verbal ways we give ourselves permission to fail. Often, should have, should not have, ought to, lead to ultimatums and emotional friction. Fixed critical views of others make them feel unappreciated.

Robin was a smart young man who sought my help because he knew he pushed others away. He worked as a computer programmer at a large company. He had no social life.

Robin: I like people, but they don't seem to like me. I see others joke and talk, but I don't seem to be able to find that. In high school and collage I just figured that I wasn't liked because I was good at school. All the people

I work with are intelligent and seem to have friends, but not me.

Dr. Phil: Any idea about how you're pushing people away?

Robin: Why do you assume that I'm at fault? Must it be my fault?

Dr. Phil: I'm not looking for fault; I'm just starting a conversation about your relationships.

Robin: I think that others don't give me a chance. Colleagues never invite me out socially, but they have no problem interrupting me and wanting help with their projects.

Dr. Phil: Do you invite others out socially?

Robin: I shouldn't have to. If they wanted me to attend their activity they should invite me.

Dr. Phil: How is that rigid view on social activity working for you?

Robin: Do you think I'm rigid? Are you simply rude, or insensitive?

Over the next month, Robin and I practiced socially acceptable ways to get him more invitations. By the end of the second month, Robin became open minded to the idea of inviting others out for coffee or lunch. At four months, Robin started dating. His life went from all work to a balance of mostly work and some play. Robin told me that, "The distraction of friends helps my work."

I find that encouraging others to make good choices helps a lot. By advocating for good choices for others, and ourselves, we bring caring people around us and encourage cooperation and kindness.

THOUGHT MINE #13: SELF BLAMING

Definition:	Feeling at fault for things that are not under your control.
Negative self-talk example:	• "I'm not exciting, he won't call me."

Couple example:	• "Why bother, no one in my family has ever gone to college. Why should I think I could." • "He wouldn't have to work so late if it wasn't for me and the kids." • "Officer, if I'd put the dinner on the table at 6 o'clock, he wouldn't have had to get so mad that he hit me. You don't understand, it's all my fault."
Teen example:	• "I don't get the math, I must be stupid."
Work/ school ex:	• "Sammy is having trouble in math. He must have gotten that from me, I hated math in school."

The act of self-blaming gives you permission to fail, and it allows others to mistreat you, without you making them responsible for their behavior. The act of blaming tends to be a distraction from solving interpersonal conflicts.

It was three days after Christmas and a family of six sat in my office. Each family member was angry and scared about the future. The four teens looked everywhere except at their father. Mom looked at her feet and cried. Eric, the father, stared straight ahead with a stern face.

"I know I blew it. I ruined everything." He said. "I didn't mean to, but I did it. I take full responsibility. I've told you all for years that I'm an alcoholic. I was just born that way. And you all know that I didn't mean to hurt anyone."

Eric had spent Christmas Eve and Christmas day in jail for drunk driving. No one in the family had slept much in days.

Eric spent most of the next half an hour explaining how he didn't want anyone in the family to be hurt by his actions. The teens tried to be supportive, but were obviously embarrassed by the fact that "…everyone was going to know." Mom added, "You could have been killed or killed someone."

When the anger and pain had a chance to dissipate, I introduced the concept of all of us being made up by the roles we play in life.

I said, "Eric, you're a father, a son, a business owner, a church member, and a person with a drinking problem. But, you are not your mistakes. You are all the parts of you that make you, you."

The family looked a little confused. So I continued, "You are not your mistakes! Everyone of us is the addition of all our parts. The accumulation of all the roles we play. Not just one role. That's why your children are scared right now. You're telling them that you're a drunk. But to them you're their dad. To your wife, you are her husband. Your family didn't fall in love with you because you are their drunk. They fell in love with all of you. And, to tell you the truth, the drunk part of you makes loving you very scary."

Self-blaming tends to make it easy to continue doing things that you wish you didn't do. Once you stop wishing, and start an action, you begin to take back self-control.

In the example above, the self-blame is complicated. Eric allowed himself to drink because he was sick. He was an alcoholic, and drinking is what alcoholics do. Eric saw alcoholism as out of his control. But once we redirected his self-responsibility to a specific behavior, Eric was able to make significant changes.

In this case, Eric focused on the behavior of avoiding drinking through a few behavior changes. He wrote the following behavior contract with his family and followed it.

1. No business meetings where alcohol was available.
2. Home at 5:30 P.M. Monday through Friday. (Make dinner Tuesday and Wednesday. Help with homework on Monday and Thursday.)
3. Movie night date with wife every Friday.
4. Saturday and Sunday afternoon fish or golf with one or more children.
5. Attend counseling with Dr. Phil weekly.

At the time of this writing, Eric chooses not to drink and freely tells people that, "… my family saved my life."

THOUGHT MINE #14: CONFUSING NEEDS WITH WANTS

Definition:	Believing that you need someone or something when it is actually just a want.
Negative self-talk example:	• "If I don't get a car, I will never get a date."
Couple example:	• "If you loved me, you'd get me that necklace." (Proof of love is a want.) • "If we have a baby, we'll start acting like a family."
Teen example:	• "If I had more friends, I'd be happy."
Work/ school ex:	• "I have to see that show tonight! Everyone will be talking about it in school tomorrow."

Often, we distract ourselves by escalating a want to a need. People need things like: water, food, clothing, housing, and safety. People also want lots of stuff like: particular cars, particular clothing, particular friends, particular jobs, and more money.

Needs tend to meet one's health and safety requirements. Wants are everything else. If we confuse the two, we are constantly in a state of emotional turmoil trying to get our wants met. Often wants are situational in nature.

Tiffy was an overly indulged teen of 17. She did not like the word "no" almost as much as her parents didn't want to say "no" to her. Tiffy's father told me that he didn't have much growing up, and he wanted better for his princes. Tiffy's mom told me, "Tiffy was a miracle baby, it took me six years to get pregnant. We almost lost her the first month. She was very frail and so small. She was a miracle baby, you know."

When I asked the parents about Tiffy, Mom said, "She is a very needy child. She doesn't like being alone. She, I suppose, is somewhat indulged. But, she hardly causes any trouble. She is a good kid."

Her father said, "Tiffy has us wrapped around her little finger. Her mother spoils her rotten. She feels guilty that we both work too much. But we do it for her. She's a good kid, but only if she gets what she wants."

I gave you this background so I could tell you about a discussion I had with Tiffy during a family therapy session.

Dr. Phil: Tiffy, you keep saying that your parents don't understand you. Can you give an example?

Tiffy: Sure can, just last night Mom got all upset with me that I didn't like a sweater she bought me. It was hideous. Green!

Dr. Phil: The green hideous sweeter was a problem because?

Tiffy: I told Mom that I need a green sweater.

Dr. Phil: You needed it for?

Tiffy: Saturday's party. I would die if I had to wear that sweater. I don't understand why she would buy that sweater for me! It was the wrong green!

Dr. Phil: You would 'Die'?

Tiffy: Well not really, but you know. I couldn't be seen dead in that sweater.

Tiffy was this dramatic about most things in her life. By making almost everything a need she was constantly in crisis mode. This family revolved around this crisis mode to Tiffy's detriment.

You may need a sweater to stay warm, but you do not need any particular color or style to survive. Style is a want. In Tiff's case, when we got down to brass tacks, she didn't like the store where mom bought the sweater.

THOUGHT MINE #15: AMBIVALENT BELIEFS

Also called:	Moral ambivalence
Definition:	Holding moral beliefs that are important to you, but carrying out behaviors that are less moral. This leads to guilt.
Negative self-talk example:	• "People who steal go to hell, but this really isn't stealing."
Couple example:	• "I liked what we did in bed last night, but girls that do that kind of stuff are sluts."
Teen example:	• "I only drank a little. Not like everyone else at the party. It's not that big a deal…"
Work/ school ex:	• "I know that sleeping around is bad, but I don't sleep with coworkers." • "Cheaters are slime, but I don't have time to read all the chapters."

Ambivalent beliefs tend to lead to feelings of guilt. Over time, unresolved guilt lowers self-esteem.

I would like to point out that ", but" (comma but) is an important sentence structure to notice. When you hear a sentence that goes, "Word word word, but…" the speaker is telling you that she does not really believe the words before the ", but".

"I really like that dress, but…" probably means, "I don't really like that dress."

Sometimes the ", but" is implied, such as in the sentence, "I believe that pre-marital sex is wrong just enough to feel guilty after I have pre-marital sex."

I once worked with a parochial school teacher who was having after school carnal activities with the school's principal—a married man. When I pointed out that she didn't seem to be living by her own moral beliefs, she replied, "I know it is wrong, but I keep telling myself that as long as his wife doesn't find out, I'm not really hurting anyone."

"You're hurting yourself." I suggest.

"Yeah, but I love him," she said, while bursting into tears.

Notice how the ", but" was used by this intelligent teacher to mitigate her own moral beliefs. Let's look at what she is really saying:

- "I know it is wrong, but I keep telling myself that as long as his wife doesn't find out, I'm not really hurting anyone."
  - [Really means] "I don't want to believe this is wrong." And "I don't care about his wife's feelings."
- "Yeah, but I love him."
  - [Really means] "I'm not really hurting myself.

THOUGHT MINE #16: SIZE PROBLEM

Also called:	Too much/too little problem
Definition:	Irrationally believing that the amount of something causes the problem or situation.
Negative self-talk example:	· "I'm too fat to take a swimming class."
Couple example:	· "Our house is too small for us to have a baby."
Teen example:	· "I have too many pimples to get a date."
Work/ school ex:	· "It's too hard to ask for a raise." · "There is no way I can get through all this homework in only a week."

Often, a person uses size problems to avoid dealing with an uncomfortable thought. When dealing with a size problem you have to define the amount, and honestly look at what that amount affects.

Mary: "I'm too fat to take a swimming class."

Dr. Phil: "How much too fat are you? What is the fattest that a person can be and still take a swimming class?"

Kevin: "Our house is too small for us to have a baby."

Dr. Phil: "What is the smallest floor space that you can live in and safely raise a baby?"

Heather: "There is no way I can get through all this homework in only a week."

Dr. Phil: "How many minutes will it take for you to do your homework?"

Often people will not use complete sentences when they throw up personal roadblocks using a size problem. For this common situation you want to ask, "_____ for what?"

Mary: "I'm too fat…"

Dr. Phil: "You're too fat for what?"

Mary: "I'm too fat to take a swimming class."

Dr. Phil: "How much too fat are you? What is the fattest that a person can be and still take a swimming class?"

Kevin: "Our house is too small…"

Dr. Phil: "Your house is too small for what?"

Kevin: "Our house is too small for us to have a baby."

Dr. Phil: "What is the smallest floor space that you can live in and safely raise a baby?

Sometimes a subject isn't a part of the opening sentence. Often all you get is a sigh or a grunt.

Heather: "There is no…"

Dr. Phil: "There is no… what?"

Heather: There is no way I can get through all this homework in only a week."

Dr. Phil: "How many minutes will it take for you to do your homework?"

Often the roadblock is just that they can't think past their perceived size problem.

The following chart may help you find Thought Mines that fit your behavior.

If the following behaviors / words sound like you	Check these Thought Mines
Exaggerate	1, 5, 12, 14, 16
Name calling	2, 7
I'm always right	3, 12
Situations are black or white, good or bad, positive or negative	3, 12
Feeling hopeless	4, 10, 13
Give up easily	4, 10, 13, 16
Often use words like: never, nothing, everything, or always	5, 10
You don't believe it when others say nice things about your skills	4, 13
The world is a half empty kind of place	6, 9, 13
Life tends to suck	6, 9, 10
Situations tend to be terrible, dreadful, shocking, awful	1, 6
Overly worry about what others think of you	7, 2
Worry about rumors	7, 13
Believe the future will suck	8
Believe the future is dangerous	8
Believe others are dumb, stupid or ill-informed	1, 9, 12
Focus on the bad in life	10
When arguing you tend to start with "I feel…"	11
Believe that you have the ability to "feel" the right answer	11
Psychic skills	11
More emotional than most	11
Often use: Should have, should not have, ought to, must, mustn't, never, have to, could have or you better	12
Unable to change your mind even with new information	12, 3, 10
Rigid	12, 3, 10
Always your fault	13, 10
I need, I have to	14
Feel out of control with money	14
If I had _____ my life would finally be better	14
History of not following own moral beliefs	15, 11
If I lose/gained weight my life would be great	16
Limit yourself do to size, amount or quantity	16, 5, 6, 1
Often feel guilty	15, 11, 7, 2

Figure 3: Thought Mines: Quick Reference Guide

ADMONITION BEFORE YOU CONTINUE

The act of noticing self-limiting thoughts puts you back in control of your future. Everyone has self-limiting thoughts. Highly effective people notice these thoughts and limit their destructive influences.

On the assumption that you have your Thought Mines under your control most of the time, you are ready to move on to the next section. However, if you do not have your Thought Mines under control, you will constantly sabotage your own goals, no matter how earnestly you want them.

LIFE REWARDS CALCULATED RISK

Richard was a nine-year veteran of a midsized police department. He consulted with me because he was unsatisfied in his work. As it turned out, he loved being a police officer, but he found that he was frustrated in his attempts to get a promotion.

"I keep missing the sergeant's exam." He explained.

"You didn't pass?" I asked.

"No, I keep missing the deadline to get my paperwork in so I can take the exam. No matter what I try, I don't seem able to get the file together so I can get it in on time."

Dr Phil: Try to pick up the cushion next to you.

Richard: What?

Dr Phil: Please, just humor me. Try to pick up the cushion.

Richard easily picked up the cushion.

Dr Phil: No Richard, I asked you to try to pick up the cushion.

Richard: What, I just did.

Dr Phil: I know you did it, but I asked you to try to pick it up.

Richard played his part and tried to pick up the cushion. He grasped it, and while making a strained face, pretended to be unable to pick it up.

Dr Phil: My point is that you either pick it

up or you don't. Try is simply a word adults use to give themselves permission to fail.

Richard: Fail?

Dr Phil: Sure. You failed to turn in the exam application didn't you?

Richard: Yeah, but not on purpose. I just ran out of time. Between work and the kids and coaching… I can't do everything!

Dr Phil: I understand that you have a lot on your plate, but by using the word try, you are giving yourself permission to fail. You either do it or you don't. Try means you didn't do it.

We need to judge ourselves by our behavior. We need to judge others by their behavior. Actions count. Intentions are merely thoughts.

I should be a multi-billionaire. That's right, billionaire — with a "B." The reason is because I invented the Frisbee when I was four or five years old and picnicking with my family at a park. I took a paper plate off the table and winged it with all my might. It was amazing. It flew! I had just invented the Frisbee. My mother was not impressed with my aeronautical skills and growled at me to stop making a mess. This scared me so much that I ran off whimpering. The newly invented Frisbee was lost in the confusion of my mind. So, if the truth were told, it is my mom's fault that I am not a multi-billionaire. Years later, some guy named, uh, Wham-o I guess, wasn't traumatized by his mother and went on to market a flying disc. He is probably a multi-billionaire.

I think it is a fair assumption that if I happened to meet Mr. Wham-o one day he would not recognize my accomplishments. I suppose he would not share his wealth with me, the true (kind of) inventor. He would probably point out that if I really was the inventor I should have patented my idea. Then I should have developed the plastic molds. I should have figured out the packaging, marketing, and the distribution of my product. I did none of that. I simply whimpered off into the poor house of obscurity.

I once heard an inventor talk about the difficulty of getting a product to market. He said, "The ideas are easy, I have them all the time. The hard part is getting others to back you with cold hard cash so you can bring the ideas to the marketplace."

The same is true in most parts of an individual's life. I have heard it a million times (at least). "I was going to…" You know what I'm talking about, the Indian tribes: the Shouldas, the Couldas, and the Wouldas. "I should have…" "I could have…" "I would have…" Probably the three leading openings of the excuse sentence are:

"I should have applied for that promotion."
"I could have invented that."
"I would have done a better job than Bob."

Other common excuse sentence starters…

"I meant to…"
"I was going to…"
"I forgot…"
"I didn't know how to start…"
"I would have done it but…"

The road of life is paved with good intentions.

Any favorites of your own?

_____
_____
_____
_____
_____
_____
_____
_____
_____
_____
_____
_____
_____

The list is huge. We love to let ourselves off the hook if we do not accomplish. Excuse making is an international pastime. I am very strict on this subject with myself. Either I did it, or I didn't do it. I am on time, or I am late. No excuses. If I am late, I messed up. It wasn't traffic or anything else. It was my lack of awareness or self-understanding. I am responsible for my life. I take this responsibility seriously.

Are you responsible for your life? Do you take your responsibilities seriously?

I am frequently told by parents, "My child doesn't act his age." The key word in this sentence is the word act. Act is the root of the word action. Life is action. We are judged by our completed actions. You either do or you don't. Do is an action,

HE FELT THAT HIS WHOLE LIFE WAS SOME KIND OF DREAM AND HE SOMETIMES WONDERED WHOSE IT WAS AND WHETHER THEY WERE ENJOYING IT.

Douglas Adams
The Hitchhiker's
Guide to the
Galaxy

Didn't Do is an inaction. Inaction is nothing. You are judged not by your intentions, but by your results. If someone runs into your car, do you care that he intended to stop? I doubt it. You judge the person by his action. (Using your car as a brake!) If your friend told you that she would pay back your loan by the end of the month so you could pay rent, does it help you pay rent if she meant to pay the loan? We are all judged by our actions.

"What have you done for me lately?" is the real world. If you are on time for work sixty-seven times in a row, great. But when you're late, does anyone really care about your sixty-seven wins? Probably not. Would your landlord care that your friend really did mean to pay you back? Or, does the landlord judge you by your actions (You didn't pay your rent on time and you loaned his money to some idiot who didn't pay you back).

If a condom works, do you really think about it much? Probably not. You just lie there thinking about how good you are in bed. But, if a condom breaks you are suddenly very attentive. Wow, you're a lot like your parents or your landlord, always focusing on the lack of appropriate action and complaining about it.

WHAT IS CALCULATED RISK?

A calculated risk is a risk that is well thought out and judged to be sound. It is a chance for you to totally screw up or to totally do well. It is not a fifty-fifty chance. That would be gambling. It is an 87.347% chance or a 92.125% chance. It is not a 100% certainty. Sometimes it is a gut feeling. Should you ask that person out? Should you apply for that new job? Should you do something that scares you?

Fear holds most people back from being amazing. Because there is a chance that they will not reach their goals, many people never attempt to reach them. And, of course, this means they never do.

Let's say you want to get to the top of a mountain to see what you can see. You can stay in your safe valley and talk about it, "I'm going to…" or you can start walking up the mountain. Let's say you only take one step. You fall and scrape your knee. Is it a loss? Definitely not. You are one step closer than you were before. You can only lose by not attempting the trek.

Let's say you work diligently. Despite attempt after attempt you only get most of the way up the mountain. Did you lose? Definitely not. You see a lot from your new skill level. The only loss would have been if you never attempted.

Life is full of examples of people that never started their lives. They never took any calculated risks. They were the same person at thirty-six as they were at thirty-five. No growth in a whole year. Now that is a loss!

I find that most people learn more from their losses than

their victories. For years I have been asking amazing people how they got to where they are in their lives. Inevitably, they talk about learning from their mistakes, picking themselves up and making a better calculated risk the next time—and the next time, and the next time, and the next time.

The loss could be love, money, work—whatever. The reality is that we learn as we go. If you stop learning I feel sorry for you. We learn through activity. We understand ourselves through activity. Without action we are not emotionally alive.

I often meet adults who are sure that they don't have a chance. They are sure that they are doomed. They say things like:

- You need money to make money.
- It's not what you know, it's who you know.
- I have no luck at all.
- My parents never talked about money when I was a kid.
- No one cared if I got good grades when I was a kid.
- I never was good at math.
- My memory isn't all that good.

Add some of your own:
- _____
- _____
- _____
- _____
- _____

Feelings of doom are inevitable with this type of self-talk. We know that self-talk needs to be questioned and controlled.

HOW CAN I DO IT DIFFERENTLY?

When life sets up a roadblock, and you fall flat on you face, you have to pick yourself up and clean off your wounds (especially the wounds to your pride). Once you're standing again, you have to ask yourself this question, "How can I do it differently?" Your job is to figure out how to calculate the way it can be done. Lots of people try to tell you why they are sure that it can't be done, but only the Smart Stubborn focus on how to do it differently.

Your power comes from looking at the problem from lots of different ways until you see a new way to get your needs met. Being a Smart Stubborn is a way to learn as you go. Gaining and reevaluating what you know, and learning how to use your accumulated knowledge, gives you power. Knowledge is maybe 10% of life. The vast majority of life is action.

The first 10%: Knowledge
>   You are or you will become what you think about the most.

The second 90%: Action
>   Without action you have nothing but inaction. Inaction is nothing.

For example, many people talk about wanting to lose weight. "Come the first of the year, I'm going on a diet." "The day after my birthday, I'm going to eat better." This self-talk is usually all talk with no action. If you listen carefully to this type of self-talk you really hear, "Not today, it isn't really important to me today. I hope it will be important to me some other day." With positive self-talk you hear yourself saying, "I walk every day. I care about myself, and walking is important to me. I am worth taking care of." When self-talk is positive, it builds upon itself.

LIFE REWARDS ACTION

I have heard it put lots of different ways, but the most succinct statement on the subject is: life rewards action. You have to choose the best action to get to your goals. If you want a good grade in History, choose to put down the Game Jerk controller and throw yourself into studying history. If you want to stop smoking, do it. Stop smoking—not at the end of this pack or on New Year's—right now! Stop. Make the words an action. If you want to stop smoking and tell yourself, "On New Year's day I will quit," you are really saying, "I will smoke until New Year's day." Action is more powerful. You need to judge yourself through your actions. You are a smoker. If you want to stop smoking, take the pack of cigarettes and crush them under your foot. Jump up and down on them, and then vacuum up the wretched mess. Now you are a nonsmoker. Act like a nonsmoker. Don't buy cigarettes. Don't ask for a cigarette. You are your actions!

If you want to get a particular job, calculate what it will take and motivate yourself to get the job. If you want to get a particular honey or hunk to notice you for the wonderful individual that you are, figure out a way to get that information imparted to them. Talk is cheap. Responsible action counts!

You also need to measure others by their actions. Their actions are the scorecard of their life. If actions are long lived they become commitment. I have a dear friend who has taught JuJitsu for forty-five years. Forty-five years, wow, that's impressive. That's commitment. It tells you something about someone who has done something for forty-five years. Even if you don't like JuJitsu, it is still impressive that anyone is committed to anything for such a long time. Commitment is the report card of your life. People believe action. I advise you to measure yourself and others by their actions. Are you willing to do what it takes to get the outcome you desire?

YOUR MORALS ARE YOUR COMPASS

I want to take a moment to talk about your morals. Morals are your sense of right and wrong. Earlier I asked, are you willing to do what it takes to get the outcome you desire? Some people read this as "anything" is OK as long as they win. I want to make this clear—I am not advocating anything goes. I am advocating pushing yourself.

John Hinkley wanted to tell Jodie Foster that he loved her, so he attempted to assassinate President Reagan. That is simply wrong. You can't do anything you want. You have to make your choices within the confines of moral behaviors.

Your morals need to be black and white. Right or wrong. I advise that you live your life 100% of the time according to your morals. When you get to that point you will be happy and proud of yourself.

Morals are not gradations. You cannot be 97% moral or 63% moral. You either are or you are not. When evaluating your own behavior, think about whether your actions are responsible and caring.

When I talk about "do what it takes" I am definitely talking about moral calculated risk. Most often it looks like more effort, more self-motivation, greater belief in yourself, and actual task completion. It never looks evil.

Morality is an absolute, not a gradation of right and wrong. Make yourself proud!

CONTROL YOUR PERCEPTIONS

When I was ten or eleven I went camping with family and friends at a state park in the Adirondack Mountains in upstate New York. On the first day we all went down to a large snow fed swimming hole. The water was very cold and I didn't like the fact that I could not see the bottom. The cold water was constantly being churned by the "buttermilk falls" that rushed down the mountainside into the picturesque pond. This place was beautiful. It had rocks on three sides, and was much larger than the public pool I was wading around in back home. I was a very new swimmer, unable to talk myself into even taking the deep end test at the pool. I had a problem. Everyone, including my stupid little brother, was having a ball, swimming to the far side of the swimming hole and jumping off the rocks. But not me. The width of the pond seemed to grow whenever I got five feet from my safe shore.

To add to my fear, fellow campers were all laughing about "How the little fish nibbled at their toes." Everyone thought it was wonderful. I wanted to go back to camp. I didn't say that however. Because, in my family, like most, (unfortunately) if they smell fear they tease you forever.

That first night around the campfire I spent most of my time furious with myself. I was sure that I was the only person who was petrified of swimming to the other side of the swimming hole.

When I was safe in my sleeping bag, I resolved to myself that the next day I was going to swim across the pond, or die trying.

By the time my slow family got to the swimming hole the morning was mostly spent. The sun was high, and the pond had grown. I steeled myself for the inevitable. I jumped into the frigid water and flailed away with my arms, kicking madly with all my might. My eyes were tightly closed. My heart was pounding.

UNDERSTANDING YOUR FEARS IS THE FIRST STEP TO CONQUERING THEM.

Cathie Black

ANY MAN WHO AFFLICTS THE HUMAN RACE WITH IDEAS MUST BE PREPARED TO SEE THEM MISUNDERSTOOD.

H. L. Mencken

I beat the water with everything I had. I was doing it. I was going to conquer the vast waters.

When I opened my eyes I was overwhelmed with despair. I was only half way. I felt panic take hold. My lungs were burning. My legs were heavy. My fingers refused to move due to the cold. I was gasping for air. I was going to die, and I didn't care.

I was nibbled on. Something had tasted my lower leg. I perked up in the water, peered through the murk to try to see the cute little fish that was playing with me. An algae covered basketball with a head bit me. Hard! A huge snapping turtle was going to devour me! I kicked at it, started to flail my arms and I didn't stop until I rammed into the rocks on the far side of the pond. I had made it. My leg was bleeding from a small bite and my hands were cut from smashing into the rocks. All that didn't matter. I was alive. Then I noticed that I had swum across (I didn't even want to think about how I was getting back).

Looking back on that incident, I am amused that I was okay with the idea of drowning, but there was no way I was going to be eaten. Being eaten motivated me, drowning didn't. Perception counts. Reality is much less important.

Our brains do not know the difference between thought and reality. You can see this at any movie theater. Moviegoers go through the full range of the emotions that the actors portray on the big screen. People lean to the left if the plane on the screen leans to the left. People feel like they are falling when the camera rushes to the edge of a skyscraper or cliff.

The *American Heritage Dictionary* defines perception as:

> Psychology - Recognition and interpretation of sensory stimuli based chiefly on memory.

The "chiefly on memory" part is what I would like to talk to you about. As we go through life we experience our world. This experience is accumulated into understanding. This understanding is a guidepost that we compare new experiences against. This comparison is the filter that our mind judges our world by. The process of filtering information through our memories is how we interpret our experiences. Thus, our personal experiences are our reality. Our reality is our perceptions and we make sense out of our world through our perceptions.

This may seem like a bunch of psycho-babble, but it's worth sticking with me on this. If our perceptions are our interpretations of the world, it must mean that how we interpret our world produces our reality. To put it simply, there is no reality, only our perception of reality. With this information we have power. We have power over the filters that interpret our reality.

No reality. What a concept! Let's look at this in the real world (sorry about the pun). Scott shows up at work to find a pink slip in his In Box. He is being let go. After five years he is unemployed. Is this a good thing, or a bad thing? The answer is neither. It is just a situation. What makes it a good or bad situation is how Scott interprets it. For all we know, Scott has been trying to find the courage to look for a new job. Maybe he was bored with his old job. But, his boss was a great guy and he didn't want to leave with this big project looming over everyone's head. This would make this pink slip a good thing.

However, if Scott recently purchased a new car with a huge monthly payment, this pink slip would be a bad thing. Scott's history filters the news into the good or bad category. News isn't good or bad, it simply is. We perceive the good or bad of it.

At this point most smart people love to prove me wrong. "What if the reality is bad, like the loss of life or something?"

It depends on how you deal with the tragic loss of life. History is full of terrible things that are forged into good.

A teen died drunk at the wheel of his parents' car. His parents had the car towed to his high school's parking lot. Through their pain they wanted the crumpled car to teach.

A seventeen-year young boy dies in a senseless motorcycle accident. His parents donate his heart, kidneys, and corneas so others can live.

Noah did nine years in prison for selling drugs. When I met him he was telling his story so others could learn. He said, "The nine years I spent in

THE SQUEAKING WHEEL DOESN'T ALWAYS GET THE GREASE. SOMETIMES IT GETS REPLACED.

Vic Gold

Philip Copitch, Ph.D.   59

prison saved my life. I have no doubt about it. If I had not gone to prison I would have died on the streets of San Francisco from the twenty years of bad choices that I had made." For most of us, nine years in prison would be perceived as bad, but for Noah, it was perceived as good.

ALS, Lou Gahrig's Disease, crippled Stephen Hawking, the preeminent mathematician and astronomer. His body is out of his control. His mother was once interviewed and she told how she worried about how he drank and played around in college and how he never applied himself. "If it wasn't for his illness he never would have taken the time to apply his mind." I am sure that Mrs. Hawking doesn't see her son's disease as a blessing. However, the way he has used his mind to advance our knowledge of the universe is definitely a blessing (and, he got to play himself in an episode of Star Trek).

This morning I awoke and turned on the radio. The newscaster was explaining "The hope is that the plane had mechanical problems and the accident was not a terrorist attack." As I learned more about the plane crash in Queens, New York, two months after the World Trade Center and Pentagon terrorist attacks, I too was hoping for accident versus terrorism. It is easier to deal with an accident than a terrorist attack. But either way, 250 people are still dead. This is a powerful example of how one's perception is controllable. If the plane crash was an accident, we could learn from it. We can make aircraft safer. But, if the crash had been a terrorist attack, we would have been dealing with planned chaos and hatred.

We all choose our own perceptions. We personally assign meaning to our world in an attempt to make sense of it. The process of assigning meaning is the use of personal filters. Our filters are learned through experiences. How you react is a choice.

CAN YOU TRUST WHAT YOU SEE?

In this section I want to show you how
easy it is for our perceptions to be tricked.

In this section I want to show you how
easy it is for our perceptions to be "tricked."

[Do you read using mostly the tops or the bottoms of the letters?]

In this section I want to show you how easy it is for our perceptions to be "tricked." We humans have five senses: sight, sound, touch, taste, and smell. Each sense can be "tricked." Due to the restraints of this book, I will mainly show illusions having to do with sight (it's really hard to trick the other senses in print).

Some of the illusions I will present will only work the first time. After you have experienced them they will never trick you again. Your mind will have learned more about your world, and you will be able to use this knowledge in the future. One time illusions are still fun. You can show them off to friends.

Some of the illusions that I will present will trick your brain every time. Even though you know the trick, you will have to figure it out every time. Chalk it up to being human, or at least an animal. Even though you know that you are being tricked you will not be able to override your perceptions. In fact, this is why I have written this section. It is important to know that you can be easily tricked even when you know there is a trick being presented. In this section you are learning how to control and understand your perceptions. Here we look at how our perceptions get tricked. I am using visual perceptions just to prove a point about perceptions in general.

Before we get started looking at vision, let me explain two tactile experiments you can try at home.

WHICH IS THE HEAVIER CAN EXPERIMENT:

What you need are three different size empty food cans, uncooked rice, and a kitchen scale. In the recycling container I found an 8 (fluid) ounce can, a 16-ounce can, and a 28-ounce can. (The remnants of some awesome slow cooked chili.) Wash and dry each can and watch for sharp edges. Fill each can with rice so that each can, along with its rice, weighs the same; 10 ounces for example. Cover each can's opening with aluminum foil.

Ask someone to pick up each can and tell you which one is the heaviest, which one is the lightest. People tend to answer that the small can weighs

I HAVE NEVER MET A MAN SO IGNORANT THAT I COULDN'T LEARN SOMETHING FROM HIM.

Galileo Galilei

the least and the large can weighs the most. Even when you tell them that each can weighs the same, they will argue. Why? This illusion is due to our expectations. We expect the small can to weigh less and the large can to weigh more. We are prepared for the weight we expect. We judge the weight through our expectations giving us our belief of its actual weight.

In my office I have a realistic looking granite rock made out of plastic. It weighs almost nothing in comparison to what a real fist sized granite rock should weigh. When people pick it up the first time they usually end up lifting it so high that they almost hit themselves in the face with the back of their own hand. Some even drop it because their perceptions are so confused.

I HAVE TO GO TO THE BATHROOM EXPERIMENT:

For this experiment you will need three bowls of water. One bowl filled with hot water, the second filled with cold water, and the third filled with room temperature water. Place the room temperature bowl in the middle. (You may wish to go to the bathroom before you do this experiment.)

Place a hand in each of the outside bowls. Let each hand get used to the hot or cold water. This usually takes about one minute. Simultaneously, place your hands in the room temperature water. Voila! You have tricked your own perceptions. Your brain gives you two different beliefs about the room temperature water, even though your brain knows the water temperature is neither hot nor cold. Don't worry about tricking your own perceptions. You do it all the time. We all do.

VISUAL ILLUSIONS:

Visual perception is the process of making sense of the reception of electromagnetic energy taken in by your eyes. Simply put, your eyes receive light waves the same way your radio receives radio waves or your television receives a television signal through a cable or from the antenna on the roof.

HUMAN BEINGS, WHO ARE ALMOST UNIQUE IN HAVING THE ABILITY TO LEARN FROM THE EXPERIENCE OF OTHERS, ARE ALSO REMARKABLE FOR THEIR APPARENT DISINCLINATION TO DO SO.

Douglas Adams
Last Chance to
See

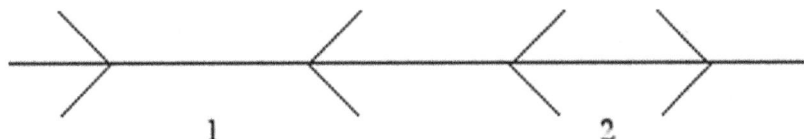

In the following illustrations you will see that your perceptions can be easily confused. Are the lines between the "> <" symbols the same, or are they different lengths?

As you can guess, line #1 and line #2 are the same length. But they do not seem to be the same length. The angle and direction of the < messes with our ability to determine the length. In the following illusions the lengths are the same, but the angles have been changed. Lines #1-6 are the same size, but they are not perceived to be the same size.

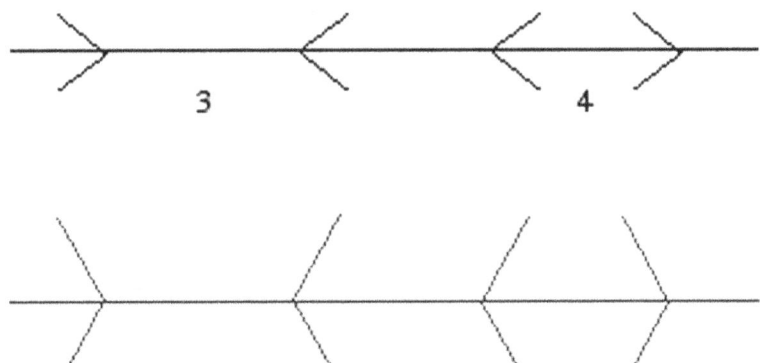

Even things you are used to seeing can be difficult to perceive if shown to you in an unusual manner:

Once you know what the above is, you will probably not be fooled by this same illusion for a long time, if ever. These are the numbers one through seven hidden by a process called symmetrical camouflage (Cover the first half of each symbol to see it easier).

In the next illusion the five balls look misaligned. If you check you will find the balls are indeed aligned. Our eyes combine the jittery effect of the lines to make the balls seem out of alignment.

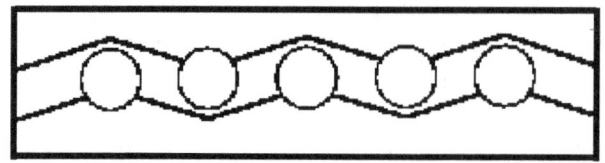

Our eyes can be tricked by misalignments and "jittery" art. The next illusion is called Jittered squares:

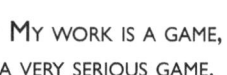

The randomly placed squares look tilted, but they are not. Feel free to use a straight edge to prove to yourself that the above squares are really aligned (this illusion is so powerful that most people have to prove it to themselves).

Illusions are what make movies work. Most people don't spend time thinking about it, but movies don't really move. We just perceive that they do.

When you watch a movie you are seeing a series of static images run back to back at a high speed. This gives the perception of motion through the process called "persistence of movement." Brothers Louis and Auguste Lumiere demonstrated the first movie in 1895 in Paris. Their demonstration showed a jockey riding a horse. Now we have British kids riding on brooms. Isn't technology wonderful?

Let's take a moment to mess with your tongue. The following is supposed to be the hardest tongue twister in the English language.

Peggy Babcock

Say it ten times fast. Ask friends to do the same so you can enjoy laughing at them.

In the next visual illusion you need to bring the image towards yourself. As you go cross-eyed, the illusion occurs.

Can you get the big fish to eat the small fish?

What do you see?

This ambiguous drawing was developed by an American psychologist named Joseph Jastrow at the start of the 1900's. Is it a rabbit or a duck? This is an example of a reversible figure that is influenced by the direction of our focus. If we focus on the left, we tend to see a duck's beak. If we focus on the right, we tend to see a bunny.[12] This figure has been shown to illustrate that the viewer's expectations are important. One study showed that on Easter Sunday children tend to see a rabbit. However during October children tend to see a duck or bird.[13]

In the next figure we see either an Eskimo looking into a cave or the silhouette of a proud Indian face (lots of little boys report seeing a boy peeing on a wall).

Our perceptions can be primed to see something that is not really there. This can be very important in criminal cases that rely on witness testimony to determine guilt or innocence. With the advances in genetic evaluation of criminal evidence we have learned that eyewitness testimony has serious drawbacks. Of the first 32 death penalty cases that were overturned by genetic testing, 28 of them had been convicted on the eyewitness testimony of credible

12- Jastrow, J. (1899). The mind's eye. Popular Science Monthly, 54, 299-312.
13- Brugger, P., & Brugger, S. (1993). The Easter Bunny in October: Is it disguised as a duck? Perceptual & Motor Skills, 76, 577-578.

witnesses.

Let's try a little priming illusion just for fun. Ask a friend to quickly repeat the word "white" ten times. When they are done, ask your test subjects, "What does a cow drink?" Don't hesitate with your question. Most people answer "milk." But, we know cows drink water! We primed the subject with his knowledge about cows. Most people think of "cows" and "milk" as synonymous.

This section was fun, but I hope I was able to prove to you that your perceptions are personal and prone to inaccuracies. This should lead you to question your own beliefs.

PURIFY YOUR FILTERS

Belief is often confused with fact. Just because you really believe something doesn't make it a fact. A fact is just that—factual. What I mean by this is that a thought that can withstand the test of repeated scrutiny is more likely to be a fact. If a thought is not questioned it is a belief, but not necessarily a fact.

So? You may be asking yourself, is this a big deal? Unfortunately, this is a big deal. If we hold onto beliefs that we do not scrutinize we are prone to develop inaccurate personal filters.

As we grow and mature we develop filters that we strain our thoughts through. When I was fifteen I would have comfortably told you that I did not like spaghetti. I was sure of it. But when I tried "real" spaghetti, spaghetti with flavor, I instantly changed my belief. My present belief is: I like home made Italian style spaghetti; I dislike canned spaghetti I got from the school cafeteria every Wednesday. If my filter (I hate spaghetti) was rigid I would not have tried real spaghetti. I wouldn't have know what I was missing out on.

Rigid filters are not challenged. This can be good or bad. I have a rigid belief that I really dislike being poked in the eye. I'm comfortable with this belief. But I need to control this rigid belief if I need eye surgery. I need to allow the surgeon to poke me in the eye for my own benefit. If we do not keep track of our beliefs and how they affect us we are being controlled by them.

Mr. Sachs was a forty-four year old businessman. He seemed physically fit. He prided himself on working hard and playing hard. During a routine insurance medical exam, Mr. Sachs was furious when his doctor wanted to give him further tests. He threw a fit and refused to have the tests that were recommended. "There is nothing wrong with my heart, I'm as fit as a horse."

Two weeks later, Mr. Sachs was taken to the hospital after complaining of chest pains. By the time he got to the hospital he was feeling better and refused treatment. He told them that he was just having heartburn and needed to get home to bed. He had a big meeting in the morning and couldn't miss it. He did agree to come in for tests the following day.

Mrs. Sachs made the appointment for her husband and forced him to go. When Mr. Sachs entered the cardiac test area he was breathing heavily and sweating profusely. He proudly told the cardiac specialist, "I don't need any tests, I'm as healthy as a horse. I just ran up and down the stairs for fifteen minutes." Mr. Sachs had done just that. To prove to his wife that she was over reacting, he had run up and down the hospital stairs.

When I met Mr. Sachs he was weak and listless. "I couldn't believe it," he whispered. "My doctor was right. I had a heart attack as they were putting on the monitoring wires. I think I would have died if I wasn't already in the hospital." Mr. Sachs damaged his heart severely. His rigid belief ("I'm as healthy as a horse") cost him seventy percent of his heart muscle and almost killed him.

You need to know how your filters influence you. Only by knowing this will you be able to use your learned filters correctly. You need to question your self-talk. It seems to be human nature that we do not notice our own shortcomings. It is difficult to be self-objective.

STAGNANT BELIEFS HOLD YOU IN THE PAST

Many people develop negative filters that are so powerful that I call them Stagnant Filters. Stagnant Filters are negative beliefs about yourself that are extremely dangerous.

Mrs. Gorman was seventy years old. She came to my office because she was depressed. She had worked as a waitress for fifty-five years and retired only when her legs would not let her do her job any longer. As I got to know Mrs. Gorman it was interesting that she had one entrenched stagnant belief through which she filtered most of her life.

Dr. Phil: It sounds like it is very hard for you to live on your social security.

Mrs. Gorman: It is. After my rent and the heat I don't have enough for my medication. I never expected to live this long so I didn't put any money away.

Dr. Phil: Any family?

Mrs. Gorman: I had a sister who died when she was twenty-eight. She had breast cancer you know. It runs in my family.

Dr. Phil: In your family?

Mrs. Gorman: My mother was a saint. She died of breast cancer when I was a little girl. My grandmother died young too, I think it was breast cancer, but no one really kept records back then.

Dr. Phil: How is your health?

Mrs. Gorman: I'm as fit as a fiddle. I'm never sick. A cold every now and then. If it wasn't for my arthritis I'd be just dandy. I never thought I would live this long, with cancer in my family and all.

Dr. Phil: Are your friends helping out?

Mrs. Gorman: To tell you the truth, I'm not a very social person. I saw people at work. I never really had friends.

Dr. Phil: You seem to like people. I don't understand.

Mrs. Gorman: It seems silly when I think about it now. But for years I have avoided making friends. I never married, but I had lots of fellas calling when I was young. It seems silly now ... but I thought I was going to die young. So I never let anyone get too close. I didn't want to hurt them. It's so hard when people you love die, you know. I thought God was going to take me any day.

Dr. Phil: Any day?

Mrs. Gorman: It sounds so silly, I know, but I always thought that I was going to die... in a day or two.

Mrs. Gorman taught me that she had lived her life waiting to wake up ill and find that she would die in a few days like her mother and sister did. Her stagnant belief kept her from making friends outside of her work acquaintances. I got to know Mrs. Gorman quite well over a few months. She was a wonderful lady with charm and grace. Unfortunately, she had been lonely for close to fifty years.

Often stagnant beliefs are imprinted on one's mind very early. Over the years I have heard lots:

- My mother always told me I was going to get fat.
- My father always said I would amount to nothing.
- I've never been good with numbers so I seem to get ripped off all the time.
- My parents liked my sister because she was the smart one.
- I only have bad luck!
- Black people are lazy (racism is a stagnant belief that undermines the individual and the community).
- Indians drink all the time.
- I couldn't learn that at my age.
- There's no one out there for me.
- I've never done that...
- No one in my family has ever...
- It's not really stealing, they won't even miss it.

LOVE IS AN ACT OF ENDLESS FORGIVENESS, A TENDER LOOK WHICH BECOMES A HABIT.

Peter Ustinov

You need to understand your own stagnated beliefs so that you can control their influence over you. Earlier we talked about questioning authority. Within yourself, your thoughts are authoritative. You need to question them. Your individual power is controlled by your own perceptions.

Any of your own stagnant beliefs cross your mind

as you read over the list above?

- _____
- _____
- _____
- _____
- _____
- _____
- _____
- _____
- _____
- _____
- _____

THE WORLD IS FULL
OF WILLING PEOPLE,
SOME WILLING TO
WORK, THE REST
WILLING TO LET THEM.

Robert Frost

DIVEST YOURSELF OF EMOTIONAL BAGGAGE

Ali entered therapy because she was getting nothing done with her life. She was thirty and spent most of her time alone. She went to work, then went to an aerobics class, then she went home. She reported that she had no social life.

When I asked her why she had no social life she replied in a matter of fact way: "I was raped by a friend in college."

She explained:

I used to be more outgoing. I went on lots of dates. When I left home and went off to school I was very active in stuff at school. I was always invited to all the parties. I got good grades and had lots of friends. At the end of the year party my sophomore year, I got real drunk. I got so drunk I really acted out. I passed out and I was raped. End of story, I was stupid. I don't even know for sure who did it. A few days later, one of the other girls told me that she knew of three guys who were bragging about the great time they had with me. I never thought that it was more than one. I sat in my dorm room and cried for the rest of the day. I went to the school counseling center and they gave me tests, but the police said that they couldn't do anything because I didn't know who raped me.

I spent the summer at home hiding. I got angrier every day. I never told my mother. She wouldn't have understood.

I told her I was unhappy and I changed schools. I thought it would be all right. I would start over.

Now I just go to work and go home. I started to gain weight, so I started doing aerobics.

After a long pause:

My life was stolen from me. I wish I could find the bastards who raped me and tell them what they did was wrong ... show them that they ruined my life, that they deserve to burn in hell. I hope they will.

Eight years later, Ali was still living the horror of her rape. She had built a prison of fear, anger, hatred, and sorrow, and locked herself within it.

EMOTIONAL PAIN LASTS MUCH LONGER THAN THE INITIAL EVENT

A large portion of the human brain has been developed to store memories. We have the ability to recall positive and negative events. Most people find that they can remember negative events better. In fact, there is lots of evidence that it was important to our very survival that we remembered negative events. The quicker a species learns from negative events, the more likely that they will survive to produce offspring. It was, and still is today, important that we learn quickly from dangerous situations. If our ancestors had not learned about the dangers, they would have been easy dinners for predatory animals.

Our minds recall negative memories with great skill. Most of the time this is probably a good thing, but sometimes we spend so much time remembering the negative, we forget to have a life. We live with one foot stuck in the past.

Research has shown that the process of thought influences the body at the system and cellular level. It is well documented that your thoughts influence your immune system, which in turn influences the way your body fights off disease.

Researchers at Ohio State University studied caregivers of Alzheimer's patients. The female volunteers agreed to have a large hole punched into the skin of their forearms. Another group of similarly aged woman, who did not take care of relatives with Alzheimer's, had the same procedure done. It is fair to say that taking care of a relative with Alzheimer's is abnormally stressful. The caregivers (abnormal stress) healed in 49 days, whereas the control group (normal stress) healed in 39 days. It took ten more days for the women who were taking care of their ill family member to heal.

In another study researchers talked dental students into having a gash put into the roof of their mouths, twice. The first cut was placed days before the dental students took their final exams, the hardest and probably most stressful exams of their lives. The second cuts were placed weeks later, after school was out. The researchers found that it took 40% longer, on average, for the pretest cuts to heal.

Another study found that when researchers deliberately squirted a cold virus into the nasal passages of volunteers, the volunteers who reported high stress levels developed the most colds. The volunteers with the lowest life stress stayed cold free. The researchers noted that test subjects that had an "avoidant-coping" style of dealing with stress stayed healthy. Positive self-talk is an avoidant-coping skill, which distracts one from the negatives in life and helps one to focus on the positives in life.

On a side note, how do researchers talk people into allowing them to cut them or stick cold viruses up their nose? I'm glad that people volunteer for scientific studies, but pity the scientist who has to ask, "Can I stick a cold up your nose, please!"

Fortunately, the immune system is less intrusive to test. Researchers at the University of New York at Stony Brook found it took only a few minutes

IT IS BETTER TO LEARN LATE THAN NEVER.

Publilius Syrus

for illness-fighting cells to decrease when college students were placed in a stressful situation. Other researchers have found that illness fighting cells are lower in people who are taking care of ill relatives, people who worry about living next to nuclear power plants, and medical students during exam week.

It seems reasonable to assume that if you are lingering in emotional turmoil you are not supporting your own overall good health. I bring this up specifically because, if you are unable to forgive, you are allowing yourself to continue the abuse ... daily. That is an awful lot of power you are giving to the aggressor from your past. Power that you are taking from yourself. Life energy that you are wasting.

FORGIVENESS IS ABOUT YOU

Forgiveness is all about you. It is about you taking control of your present and future life. When Ali decided that she was not going to allow her life to be controlled by her pain and misery, she regained her life. When Ali took her pain and made it into a positive action, she started the road to self recovery.

When she was being consumed by hate she said:

> My life was stolen from me. I wish I could find the bastards who raped me and tell them what they did was wrong ... show them that they ruined my life. That they deserve to burn in hell. I hope they will.

When she forgave:

> Once I realized that forgiveness was for me, that I deserved not to feel the hate any longer, I started to look at ways I could take control of my life. I decided that I needed to feel safer. I made a rule for myself that I would never drink to where I was out of control. Now I will have a beer or two, but I am always aware of my surroundings. I took a self defense class at the YMCA and thought a lot about

THE BEST THING TO GIVE TO YOUR ENEMY IS FORGIVENESS; TO AN OPPONENT, TOLERANCE; TO A FRIEND, YOUR HEART; TO YOUR CHILD, A GOOD EXAMPLE; TO A FATHER, DEFERENCE; TO YOUR MOTHER, CONDUCT THAT WILL MAKE HER PROUD OF YOU; TO YOURSELF, RESPECT; TO ALL MEN, CHARITY.

Francis Maitland Balfour

how to be aware of my surroundings. One interesting thing about the self defense class I took was learning all the ways I can protect myself way before having to fight off an attacker.

I also had a heart to heart talk with my sister. She is three years younger than me and I wanted to make sure that she didn't get into the same trouble I got into. We took the class at the Y together.

Forgiveness needs to go from a thought to a behavior. You never say what the aggressor did was OK with you, you just know, deep within yourself, that you will not let them continue to control you through your own fears. The types of forgiveness behaviors are very personal. Some find that the behavior must be grand; while others find that subtle behaviors work best for them. It will depend on your personality. Forgiveness behavior is never revenge.

FORGIVENESS BEHAVIORS THAT HAVE WORKED FOR OTHERS

The following is a list of forgiveness behaviors that others have found to work for them. It is in no particular order. Forgiveness needs to become a behavior, but that behavior is very personal.

Smaller issues such as when someone wrongs you:

- Avoid the offending person. Know that they don't warrant your attention.
- Learn to recognize this type of person so that they can be avoided sooner.
- Forgive and then forget, move on.
- Write a letter—mail it or not.
- Talk to the person who wronged you, calmly explaining that you do not allow people to treat you that way.

Bigger issues such as when someone violates you:

- Call the police and make a formal report.
- Attend a victims' group.
- Write an article that will help others.
- Talk to a loved one, sharing what you have learned.

YOU CAN KNOW THE NAME OF A BIRD IN ALL THE LANGUAGES OF THE WORLD, BUT WHEN YOU'RE FINISHED, YOU'LL KNOW ABSOLUTELY NOTHING WHATEVER ABOUT THE BIRD... SO LET'S LOOK AT THE BIRD AND SEE WHAT IT'S DOING -- THAT'S WHAT COUNTS. I LEARNED VERY EARLY THE DIFFERENCE BETWEEN KNOWING THE NAME OF SOMETHING AND KNOWING SOMETHING.

Richard Feynman

THERE IS NO REVENGE SO COMPLETE AS FORGIVENESS.

Josh Billings

Philip Copitch, Ph.D. 75

- Help others who are less fortunate than yourself.
- Take a self-defense class.
- Write a letter—mail it or not.
- Talk to the person you are focusing on and tell them that you forgive them (with or without them understanding what this means).

What can you do for you?

- _____
- _____
- _____
- _____
- _____
- _____
- _____
- _____
- _____
- _____
- _____
- _____
- _____
- _____
- _____
- _____
- _____
- _____
- _____
- _____
- _____
- _____
- _____
- _____
- _____
- _____

LIFE IS AN ADVENTURE IN FORGIVENESS.

Norman Cousins

- _____
- _____
- _____
- _____
- _____
- _____
- _____
- _____
- _____
- _____
- _____
- _____
- _____
- _____
- _____
- _____
- _____
- _____
- _____
- _____

FORGIVENESS IS ALMOST A SELFISH ACT BECAUSE OF ITS IMMENSE BENEFITS TO THE ONE WHO FORGIVES.

Lawana Blackwell
The Dowry of Miss
Lydia Clark

Your goal is to obtain emotion closure. This is shrink speak for bringing an end to your emotional involvement. When you are emotionally done with the individuals who hurt you, the hurt stops. You no longer have an emotional need to focus backward, freeing you to focus on you and your future. Emotional closure is emotional freedom.

TO CLOSE THIS CHAPTER, A FEW MORE TONGUE TWISTERS:

3 times fast: Soldiers Shoulders

3 times fast: Red leather, yellow leather

A cup of proper coffee in a copper coffee cup.

Sally saw Sylvester stacking silver CD's side
  by side.

<u>A French tongue twister:</u>

Un chasseur sachant chasser sait chasser
sans son chien de chasse.

<u>A Hebrew tongue twister:</u>

Shelama Shlomo Shalem Simla Shlaima?

שלמה שלמה שלמה שלמה

"I'll be a few minutes late... I have to stop by my ex-wife's house..."

"According to the divorce settlement, I still have to take out the garbage."

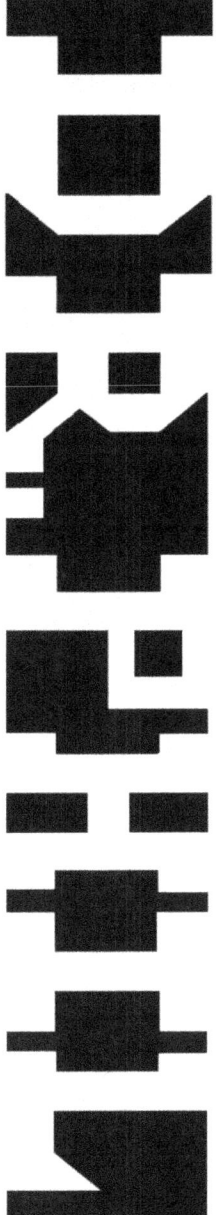

THIS IS A FORM OF REVERSE ART. MOST PEOPLE NOTICE THE DARK VERSUS THE LIGHT (NON) PRINT AREAS.

"Welcome class...It is my goal that by the end of the year
you will understand the New Yorker cartoons."

3. UNDERSTANDING GOAL SETTING

As far back as 1935, motivation and incentive learning has been studied. Cecil Alec Mace was a British philosopher and psychologist who studied how the type of goal influenced performance.[14] In the 1950's, John W. Atkinson took an analytical view in his edited work, *Motives in fantasy, action and society*.[15] It wasn't until the end of the 1980's that industrial and organizational psychologists began studying goal setting from multiple directions.[16]

Simply put, goal setting is the act of picturing what you want with microscopic clarity. Unfortunately, most people do not obtain their goals because of one of two reasons.

1. They do not have clear goals.
2. They give up as soon as an obstacle gets in their way.

However, when you ask them what happened to their goal, they tend to blame everyone or everything other than themselves. The reverse of this is when this same person talks about another's success. You know what they say, "He was lucky."

Highly effective people do not believe in luck when it comes to success. Highly effective people make thousands of well thought out decisions, develop strategies, follow plans, and stick to their goals. Then, years later, their brother-in-law says about them, "That Bob, he sure is damn lucky!"

What I have noticed is that in America opportunity, not only knocks, it practically bashes down the door trying to get attention. When opportunity finally does get someone's attention, they can't figure out how to open the door, or if they do get the door open, they are uncertain about what to do next. They stand in the doorway looking opportunity right in the face and don't know what they are gazing upon.

14- Mace, C. A. (1935). Incentives: Some experimental studies (Report No. 72). London: Industrial Health Research Board.
15- Atkinson, J. (1958). Towards experimental analysis of human motivation in terms of motives, expectancies and incentives. In J. Atkinson (Ed.), Motives in fantasy, action and society (pp. 288-305). Princeton, NJ:Van Nostrand.
16- Locke, E. A., & Latham, G. P. (1984). Goal setting: A motivational technique that works! Englewood Cliffs, NJ: Prentice Hall.

The problem is that most people don't know that opportunity shows up in the rough. They stand at the door, looking at this ragamuffin and converse with it:

Opportunity: Hi goal seeker, I'm glad you found me.

Goal seeker: Are you a hobo or something?

Opportunity: No, I'm opportunity and I came a-knocking.

Goal seeker: No seriously, are you homeless? Destitute?

Opportunity: No, I'm not kidding, I'm opportunity.

Goal seeker: You can't be opportunity!

Opportunity: Why not?

Goal seeker: Well, nothing personal, but you don't look like you have two nickels to rub together, let alone the millions I'm seeking. You look… well kind of like a ragamuffin.

Opportunity: What did you expect me to look like?

Goal seeker: Like opportunity, all spit shined, with jewels and maybe a tux.

Opportunity: Oh, I see. I think you have me confused with luck.

Goal seeker: Luck?

Opportunity: Oh yes indeed, I always show up in work clothes and you have to provide your own luck. When I show up, I'm a diamond in the rough. You have to shape me, grind me, polish me, nurture me, and love me.

This is a little known fact; opportunity knocks many times in a lifetime. You have to notice the knocking and open the door. And when you open the door, expect opportunity to be wearing work clothes. Opportunity is a work in progress; you have to roll up your sleeves and progress.

So, let's move forward, next we will cover the pitfalls that keep people from obtaining their goals.

AVOIDING THE PITFALLS

We are often our own worst enemy. Along with the Thought Mines discussed earlier, we often carry personal fears deep in our psyche. In this section, we will look at how to avoid this mess and get on with getting your goals met.

Cathie Black, in her book *Basic Black*, discusses fear in her experience in the newspaper and magazine publishing business.[17]

> Fear—fear of someone's reaction, fear of unexpected consequences, fear of failure—is a very real part of the work experience, and learning how to deal with it is one of the most empowering skills you can develop. In fact, you can learn not only to neutralize the harmful aspects of fear, but turn it around and use it for your benefit.

TROUBLE IS ONLY OPPORTUNITY IN WORK CLOTHES.

Henry J. Kaiser

AVOID THE FEAR OF FAILURE

Noted psychoanalyst, Harry Stack Sullivan, devoted his career to the study of interpersonal relationships. Dr. Sullivan taught that there are two generic causes for fear. The first, is that threat is either perceived or imminent. The second, is novelty.

Sullivan's first category is easy to understand. People are afraid of being attacked, physically or emotionally. The second category is subtler and more important to our present conversation. Sullivan noted that people are fearful of something new, something less known or understood by them.[18] Simply, people don't handle change well.

DEFINE YOUR BUSINESS GOALS CLEARLY SO THAT OTHERS CAN SEE THEM AS YOU DO.

George Burns

In an article in Psychology Today, *Embracing the Fear of Failure*, Frank Pittman discusses the fear of failure within the context of getting married.[19]

Look at the craziness of what we spend

17- Black, Cathie. Basic Black: The Essential Guide for Getting Ahead at Work (and in Life), Crown Business. New York. 2007
18- Sullivan, H.S. The Interpersonal Theory of Psychiatry. W.W. Norton, 1953.
19- Embracing the Fear of Failure Breaking out of your comfort zone and facing your mistakes can lead to innovation and stronger relationships. Carlin Flora http://psychologytoday.com/articles/pto-20041026-000001.html.

on weddings to try to make something spotless and flawless to start off the relationship.

And yet, you can be sure there will be a good fight and bad sex within 24 hours.

Pittman says that rather than working to achieve romantic perfection, people must learn to survive reality together. Failure is not the issue. How you deal with it is.

When I was a much younger, and if you don't mind me saying—thinner therapist, I was assigned a teen group of juvenile delinquents with drinking problems. As excited as I was with having a job, I was unsure of how to deal with the inevitable question, "What do you know about my problems?"

On the first day, I joined the established group in the dingy cinder block room of a locked facility. The therapist who was turning the group over to me suggested that I introduce myself at the appropriate time. The folding chairs were positioned in a circle, and sixteen seemingly angry teens glared at each other. In typical AA fashion we went around the room each saying our names. "Hay, I'm Sawbone and I'm an alcoholic." "I'm Robby and I'm an alcoholic." When it got to my turn I said, "Good morning, I'm Phil and I'm a professional failure." My confession lead to my explanation and eventually to an enthusiastic group discussion about our fear of failure. What I explained to the group was that I was a pro at failing. I had failed large and small. But, I was not my mistakes. I had failed a lot, but I was not a failure.

It is important to know, in your heart, that failure is a group of actions that ends up with an unexpected outcome. Failure is not a character flaw. Your plan can fail, but you cannot. Well, that is not entirely accurate. You cannot fail until you give up. If you learn from the failure, the failure was simply an obstacle unforeseen by your plan to get to your goal.

I saw an interview with J. K. Rowling of Harry Potter fame. She explained that her first book, *Harry Potter and the Sorcerer's Stone*, was rejected five times. Publishers thought the story line was too complicated for young readers. I hear she has sold a few books over the years. What if she only sent

IN THE MIDDLE OF DIFFICULTY LIES OPPORTUNITY.

Albert Einstein

IT IS YOUR WORK IN LIFE THAT IS THE ULTIMATE SEDUCTION.

Pablo Picasso

the book to four publishers and gave up?

Fear is part of the human condition. What you do with the fear, is what counts. Fear stops most people before they start.

KNOWLEDGE

To get out of your comfort zone you will need new information. You need information that expands your comfort zone. The lack of knowledge leads to fear, thus the addition of knowledge deceases fear. With enough knowledge fear can be virtually eliminated.

Mary had a nice home across from an elementary school. She played with the idea of opening a day-care center. She played at it for five years. When I discussed with her that fear was holding her back she adamantly denied it. "I'm not afraid of anything, I just don't know how to open a day-care center. All those forms and regulations!"

Dr. Phil: What would you do if you weren't afraid?

Mary: I'd take a course at the community college! (She snapped back at me.) Oh, my gosh, I'm so sorry, I guess I am a little afraid.

As it turned out, the local college offered a weekend class that explained the process in great detail. Mary spent $35 to get the knowledge, as well as the forms and contacts that she needed to open her day-care program.

This story illustrates a phenomenon that I have seen time and time again. Often people know what they need to know and where they need to go to get started.

One young man told me that he wanted to be a state licensed contractor and he thought he could pass the state contractors' test. After numerous attempts to get a straight answer from him concerning what he needed to do to prepare for the state test he said, "I guess I just have to go into the closet and get out the box."

As it turned out, almost a year before, he had bought a home study course. His fear of failure kept

HALF OUR LIFE IS SPENT TRYING TO FIND SOMETHING TO DO WITH THE TIME WE HAVE RUSHED THROUGH LIFE TRYING TO SAVE.

Will Rogers

OPPORTUNITY IS MISSED BY MOST PEOPLE BECAUSE IT IS DRESSED IN OVERALLS AND LOOKS LIKE WORK.

Thomas A. Edison

YOU CREATE YOUR OPPORTUNITIES BY ASKING FOR THEM.

Patty Hansen

him from opening the box.

These two examples seem pretty easy. But to the people involved their fear stagnated them. When the goals are extremely complicated you have to break the situation into bite size tasks.

An old proverb asks, "How do you eat an elephant?" The answer, "One bite at a time." If you try to eat an elephant all at once, by hauling it up with a crane and dropping it whole into your mouth, you're one smushed diner. But, if you carve it up you can get it done. If you bite off more than you can chew, you spit it out and cut the piece smaller, then get back to chewing.

When it comes to obtaining the knowledge you need, you may have to cut it up into lots of small pieces that may take years to digest.

Miguel had just turned twenty-seven, and according to the school's schedule, was less than a year away from earning his Ph.D. in chemistry. The problem was that he was six months into his doctoral dissertation write up and had accomplished a week's worth of work. He was concerned that he was going crazy.

As it turned out, he started almost every day off with a great plan—work on his dissertation write up. He had all his lab research done, and now he only had to do what he thought would be the easy part. He just had to write a few hundred-page report with impeccable documentation and career altering ramifications.

Miguel began his day with a simple plan, get up and have a small breakfast. After breakfast hit the books. But something always got in the way. He explained:

> This morning for example, I was eating breakfast and I noticed the plants in the backyard needed watering. So I watered them. When I was watering the plants I noticed that the car looked a little dirty so I needed to wash it. While I was at the car wash I decided to get the oil changed at the place on the corner. It only took twenty minutes. After that I was feeling a little hungry. So I stopped at a local sandwich shop. I only played a few games of chess with my friend, Barry. After the

COURAGE IS RESISTANCE TO FEAR, MASTERY OF FEAR - NOT ABSENCE OF FEAR.

Mark Twain

games we realized—why bother going to the library since it was already 3:30? So Barry, he's also working on his dissertation, and I decided to get some stress relieving exercise. We went and tossed a Frisbee down by the commons.

What Miguel (as well as Barry) needed was knowledge on how to formulate a better plan of attacking this huge project. Miguel did great when a professor was setting the agenda. But when Miguel had to set his own agenda fear of failure took over.

Miguel was stuck. What if he couldn't get his dissertation completed on time? You can tell by his behaviors that it was easier to get little "nothing" tasks completed, versus little "something" towards his important goal.

Once Miguel and I broke his dissertation into small, chewable chunks, he settled down to work.

TWO WAYS TO GET KNOWLEDGE

IMAGINATION IS MORE IMPORTANT THAN KNOWLEDGE...

Albert Einstein

The old saying, "Knowledge is power" is true as far as it goes, but misleading. The implication is that you need to personally have the knowledge. The fact is that what you need is an organized mind that can obtain knowledge. There are two ways to deal with knowledge:

1. LEARN IT YOURSELF:

As in the examples above, you can learn what you need to know. But often, that is not necessary. The act of learning is time consuming and takes interest. You will need to learn how to obtain your goal. Expertise that is not directly related to your goal is often not worth your time and effort to learn.

2. HIRE IT, RENT IT, OR TRADE FOR IT:

Often it is easier and cheaper to hire the knowledge you need. Don't get caught into thinking you need to know everything to obtain a goal. If the goal is impressive, the skills needed to obtain it will be impressive.

I understand my business inside and out. But I hire an accountant to watch the money. I often joke

"I am only afraid of two things, cancer and the IRS. I just don't know which I fear the most."

There is no way I can keep up with the IRS regulations, the payroll regulations, and the city, state, county, and federal forms. So I hire a tax wizard to watch my back.

You need to be able to make use of the knowledge, but you don't have to have the knowledge personally.

ARE YOU WILLING TO DO WHAT IT TAKES TO GET THE OUTCOME YOU DESIRE?

I would like to start off with a big fat warning. The above doesn't mean: Are you willing to do whatever it takes to get the outcome you desire at any cost? Screw everyone else! I am not advocating that you can do anything just because you want something. That's stupid. I'm stating that you are responsible for your actions and better use heaps of forethought before you initiate a plan. I once received a fortune cookie that read: "A bad person is a good example of a bad example." As discussed in Chapter 2, morals concerning right and wrong must be incorporated into doing whatever it takes.

A perfect example of this bad example was in today's paper. The lead article of the local section was titled: *Suspect - Shooting was an accident.* The subtitle read: Redding teen pleads innocent to charges from robbery attempt.

As in other sections of this book, I have changed the name of the person involved. The article was about 18 year-old Albert Whole; A. Whole for short. It was explained in the paper that A. Whole "…told police he didn't mean to shoot a gas station clerk during a robbery attempt."

A. Whole's sister was quoted, "He's a good kid. He made bad choices."

The article continued:

> The shooting at the Grease Street gas station came four days after A. Whole's friends allegedly burglarized a Shasta Lake home on Thanksgiving Day, stealing as many as 10 guns, A. Whole told police.
>
> A group of four friends, including A. Whole, had talked about robbing a bank sometime in the next year, he told police.

They spoke of using automatic weapons, grenades and rocket launchers, he said.

But, A. Whole decided to rob the gas station on his own he said, because he owed money to probation officials and didn't want to go back to prison.

So, A. Whole said he waited outside the station for two hours to see if the clerk would leave his booth. About 3:30 AM, he finally threw a rock at a parked car to get the attendant's attention, reports said.

The clerk emerged and A. Whole appeared with a gun and demanded money, he said. The attendant refused, and the gun accidentally went off, the suspect said.

The gas station attendant suffered serious injuries.

In the story above, A. Whole worked it out in his mind that this was a good choice. He didn't think about right and wrong. He didn't think about the gas station attendant. He stayed focused on his problem and gave himself permission to disregard everyone else's needs. This selfish lack of insight is often confused with freedom, but in actuality it is simply stupidity.

WE NEED TO QUESTION OURSELVES

As we take on adulthood we need to constantly question our own authority. We need to look at the bigger picture of our lives.

A few good self-questions are:

- Would I be proud of this behavior if it was explained on the front page of the newspaper?
- Would I feel right if I had to explain my behavior to _____? (Fill in the name of someone you truly respect and would not want to embarrass yourself in front of).
- Would I want someone to do this to me, or someone I love?
- Would I do this if I knew I was going to be caught?
-

KNOWLEDGE IS POWER.

Sir Francis Bacon

KNOWLEDGE IS OF TWO KINDS. WE KNOW A SUBJECT OURSELVES, OR WE KNOW WHERE WE CAN FIND INFORMATION ON IT.

Samuel Johnson

These self-governing moral questions help us make good decisions, even when we want to do whatever initially crossed our minds.

CONFIDE IN YOURSELF AND CHOOSE YOUR COUNSEL WELL

Often when we want to change something in our world we bounce the emerging idea off others. This sounding board notion is both good and dangerous. It is good to seek out counsel and listen carefully to competent advice. It makes sense to talk to a highly experienced plumber if you are thinking about going into the plumbing trade. It makes sense to learn as much as possible about a business before you choose to apply for a job. But, when you gather information you need to be aware that the giver of the information is filtering her answers through her own life experiences. You need to judge the filters of others.

I once told my Uncle Joe that I was thinking of applying for a doctoral program in psychology on the other side of the country. His words were very specific. "Listen to me boy, you're a poor kid from Rottenchester, how are you getting into grad school?" He continued to explain that school was great for rich kids who buy a fancy piece of paper. He was positive that "people like us" had to make money with our hands.

I have often thought about Uncle Joe's advice. If I had not understood his filters I would probably be a businessman in Rochester, New York. There is nothing wrong with that, but it wouldn't have been my choice. I wanted to be a shrink.

Gathering information is imperative to making good choices. Over the years I have found books to be very helpful in giving me solid information. I am very choosy however. I tend not to believe any author who is trying to sell me something other than the information. Be super careful with diet books, make-money-quick books and books that tell you that they know what God is thinking.

WHEN I'M WORKING ON A PROBLEM, I NEVER THINK ABOUT BEAUTY. I THINK ONLY HOW TO SOLVE THE PROBLEM. BUT WHEN I HAVE FINISHED, IF THE SOLUTION IS NOT BEAUTIFUL, I KNOW IT IS WRONG.

R. Buckminster Fuller

ADAPT OR STAGNATE

You need to scare yourself a little bit on a regular basis. If you are not nervous every now and then, you are sitting comfortably inside your safety zone. That may be safe, but it is not living. As we talked about in the last chapter, life rewards action. You have to be doing or you are stagnant. Cesspools are stagnant and like cesspools, people begin to stink up the place when they stagnate.

The best question I know to stop stagnation is: How can I do it differently? How can I do it differently? How can I do it differently? How can I do it differently? How can I do it differently? How can I do it differently? How can I do it differently? How can I do it differently? How can I do it differently? How can I do it differently? How can I do it differently? How can I do it differently?

The preceding is not a typo. You need to ask yourself, "How can I do it differently?" Over and over, until you have lots of choices to work with. With lots of choices you have the best chance to have a great choice in front of you. If you have only one or two choices you may not have any really good ones on your plate. The great choice may not show up until you have challenged your mind 47 times (or some such number). With 47 options to muddle through you have real comparisons. You have stuff to appraise so that you can calculate your risks.

Melissa is ill with cancer. She has three children in their teens. She told me, "It really makes me angry when people say, 'You're so strong, taking care of your kids when you have cancer.' What am I supposed to do, sit around and wait to die? I do what I have to do. I take care of my family."

Melissa is a caring individual who takes pride in her life choices. She has taught me that she is stuck with cancer, but she isn't stuck without choices. She asks herself regularly, "How can I do it differently?" on little tasks that you and I take for granted. Melissa is in control of her life.

A homework assignment:

On the following page write the first letter of your name. Now ask yourself the question, "How can I do it differently?" and draw that same letter differently. Then ask yourself the question, "How can I do it differently?" Ask it again, and again. Fill the page with different letters (for you computer types you may notice that you are changing fonts).

It is the same letter with a different outcome each time.

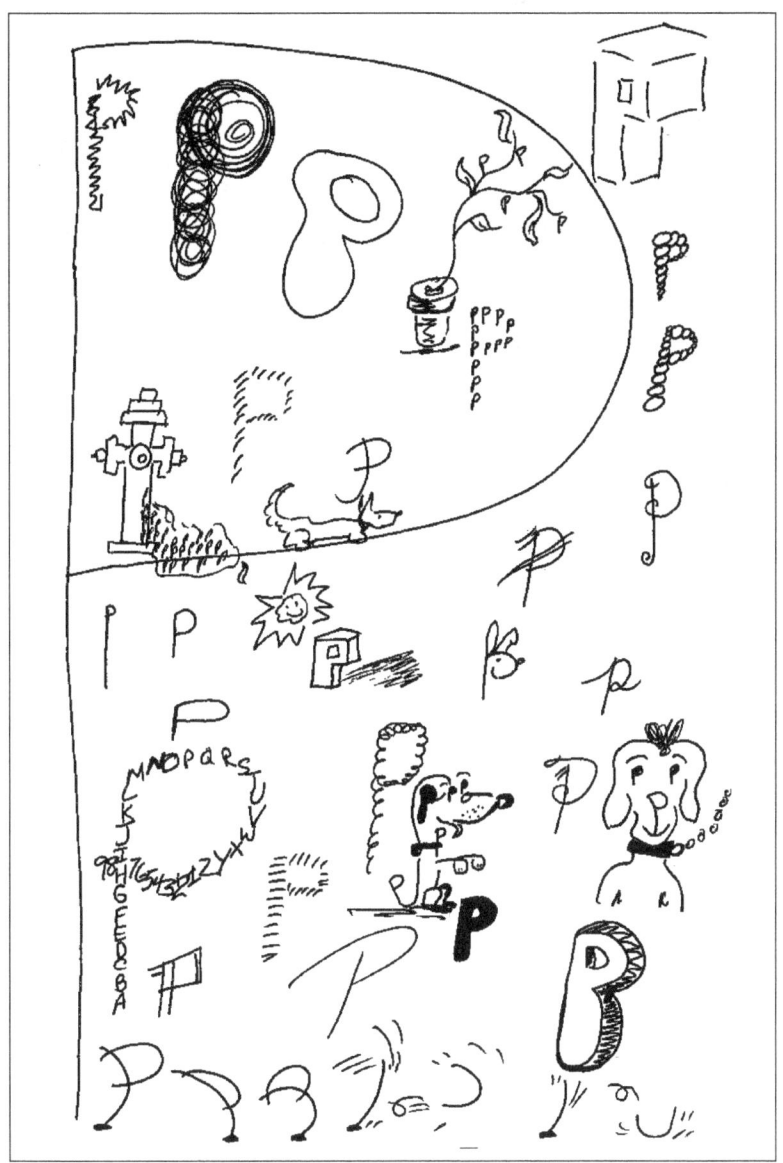

My view of the letter P

I suspect that with each new font you will find it getting harder and harder. At letter number 25 you are probably forging new ground and taxing your mind. Attempt number 30 would not have occurred without the 29 before it. This is an example of how to expand your mind to find a new way to do something you already know.

ONE CHOICE AT A TIME

If you choose to go to the movies, you are actually choosing not to do an infinite number of other things you could be doing instead of going to the movies. By choosing to go to the movies you are choosing not to feed the homeless, not to go for coffee, not to do your philosophy homework, not to… you fill in the blank. Usually, you can only make one choice at a time. But, often one choice has a ripple effect on numerous other choices. A. Whole chose to rob a gas station that led him to jail. I think that most people his age chose to sleep at 3 AM. This probably wasn't seen as much of a choice. But if A. Whole had chosen to go to bed that fateful night, he wouldn't have chosen to shoot an innocent man.

MOST PEOPLE AND WATER TAKE THE PATH OF LEAST RESISTANCE

Water takes the path of least resistance. It slowly erodes the ground and over time creates a rut. Add more time and water and it forms a stream. After enough time and enough water you end up with a wondrous tourist destination—the Grand Canyon. As we spoke of before, lots of small choices lead to accomplishments. The Grand Canyon was formed from raindrops and commitment to a path.

We humans are going to do something. We are like the raindrops. We are going to be. If we take our little choices and combine them, we become a force. Unlike a river, we are not stuck following the path of least resistance. We can take calculated risks and focus our life force towards a planned goal. If you don't know where you're going—you're there. You're stagnant. If you can adapt, you have a future.

TAKE THE ATTITUDE OF A STUDENT, NEVER BE TOO BIG TO ASK QUESTIONS, NEVER KNOW TOO MUCH TO LEARN SOMETHING NEW.

Og Mandino

4. UNDERSTAND HOW TO CONTROL TIME

In this section we will look at how our nature towards inactivity and distractibility gets in our way. Simply put, how we manage (or probably mismanage) our time.

For many, the word "manage" denotes following rules and being controlled. For countless adults, being managed is being told what to do. Who wants to be told what to do? I would like to look at this differently.

The word "manage" means: To direct or control the use of. In this chapter we are going to focus on self-direct and self-control. We are going to learn how to control time and use it, versus being controlled by it and subservient to it.

British academic and writer, C.S. Lewis wrote,

> The Future is something which everyone reaches at a
> rate of sixty minutes an hour, whatever he does, whoever
> he is.

This may seem like a basic truism, but most people lie to themselves about this fact. Let's separate fact from fiction.

The Fact: We calculate time on planet Earth based on our planet's rotation. One day equals 24 hours. One hour equals sixty minutes. One minute equals sixty seconds. If you do the math, there are 86,400 seconds in a day - everyday. No more, no less. Everyone gets the same amount. 86,400 little parts of every single day. [60 seconds X 60 minutes X 24 hours/day= 86,400 seconds.]

But: Some people get a lot more done in 86,400 seconds than other people get done.

Why: The simple answer: choice. Most people choose to waste time and they do it by not paying attention to their lives or by lying to themselves about time. Let's look at how we lie to ourselves.

TIME LIES

There are three major lies we use to trick ourselves concerning time.

1. There is more time in the future.
2. I don't care about time.
3. You can "save time."
4. There is more time in the future.

1. THERE IS MORE TIME IN THE FUTURE.

Ever find yourself saying, "I'll do it later"? This assumes that later has more time in it than now. Somehow, in your future you have this large chunk of time sitting around waiting for you to catch up to it and use it. My friend Snyder often jokes, "I'll do it in my spare time or my extra time." She is joking about the fact that there is no "extra time" or "spare time." There are only 86,400 seconds in our day. You can't save it up for later. You can't buy more from a clock shop. You can't find more under the bed or in the pocket of an old pair of jeans (which are probably under your bed).

It is important to know that you have only so much time. Time may be infinite, but you are not. You may live 80 years, which is a lot in comparison to the average housefly. But, 80 years is pretty much nothing in the existence of a small class M planet circling around a nothing-small yellow star in the dull outer corner of the cosmos. Your life goes by with or without you paying attention.

2. I DON'T CARE ABOUT TIME.

Recently, my fourteen-year-old son announced, "I'm bored, there's nothing to do!" I did my dad thing and asked, "What do you want to do?" "I dunno, everything is boring." he said as he flopped hopelessly onto the couch. "I know," he continued. "Life can't be boring, only people can be boring." He knows me so well. He used my line before I got to. But, life can't be boring, it just is. What you do with life is what makes it boring or exciting. So, if someone is bored, I'm sure they are boring. They need to do something.

If you are unconscious about time it simply ticks away. It doesn't care about anything. It just is. What makes time valuable is what you do with it.

In our society we punish criminals by making them "waste" time. We put them in jail. We give them boredom as a punishment. I often see people who place themselves in self-imposed jails of thought in which their life goes by with little self-awareness or personal growth. What a waste. Personally, during the big dirt nap I'll waste all the time I could ever wish to waste. While I'm alive, I want to live.

Caring about time has to be a conscious choice.

3. YOU CAN "SAVE TIME."

You can't take a jar of time and put it on a shelf for a later date. Everyday you get your allotment of 86,400 seconds. What you do with it is your choice. Use it wisely or not, at the end of 86,400 seconds the day is over and you're onto your next allotment. What most people mean when they say "saving time" is that they want to do something in less time, leaving more time to do something else.

I find myself trying to "sleep fast" so I can get onto my next set of 86,400 seconds. I don't want to use a lot of seconds sleeping, even though I know that without quality sleep, my awake time is less fulfilling.

I want to drive the shortest way most of the time, so I have time to do something else with the time "saved" from driving the long way. All this word play really means is that I want to get the most done in the shortest amount of time so I can still do more. What we are talking about is efficiency.

The word efficient comes from the old English word, dhe that means, "do." So for a really long time, humans have known that you have to do to get anything done (your ancestors were brilliant). Once you understand that you need to do, the problem becomes how. What are the ways to do things more efficiently? This will be discussed later, but first let's focus on what to avoid; how to protect ourselves from the dreaded Time Bandits.

TIME BANDITS

Time Bandits is not just the name of a cool English flick from 1981. Time Bandits are things in our lives that rob us of time. Time crooks! The opposite of wasting time is using time efficiently. This big question is really two questions. What to do and what not to do? To answer this we have to look at the negative side of this equation—what not to do. What do we need to avoid, in order to get our stuff done? This time stuff can give you a headache.

The key things to avoid:

ATTITUDE

Attitude is a state of mind or a feeling, from the Latin word, aptitd that means faculty. Faculty means an inherent power or ability. So what this means to us is that our attitude is personal to us and is inseparable from us. We control our attitude; it defines our character, we are our attitude.

I believe it is attitude that holds most people back and makes most people unhappy and unfulfilled. When it comes to time and attitude I want to tell you a story. The following story is about a high school student with an attitude problem. What is interesting is that this kid is really no different than many adults with "attitude problems."

Dale is a smart kid who ended up at my office after earning straight 'C's' in his junior year of high school. His parents were not happy that he wasn't trying, and constantly bombarded Dale with the old tired line, "You have so much potential."

When I met with Dale he explained, "I hate home-work… it's boring and useless. It takes too much time for no real reward!"

To get his parents off his back, Dale agreed that he would commit 1 1/2 hours to homework on school nights as long as his parents didn't hover over him or talk to him about "his potential." His parents also agreed.

I met with the family a week later and Dale was very upset with the agreement he had made with his parents. Everyone was honoring their part of the agreement, but Dale was angry that he wasn't able to get his homework done in 1 1/2 hours. He was very upset that his school was giving him so much "lame" homework.

I suggested that Dale videotape himself doing his homework. My plan was for Dale to do his homework for 1 hour and to spend the next half hour viewing the video to see how much time he was wasting and not really doing his homework. It is my contention that lots of time is wasted during homework periods that people don't realize they are wasting. The next week the family and I came together and Dale was happy to inform me that he didn't watch any of the tapes.

Dr. Phil: How come, I thought you agreed to watch the tape?

Dale: I didn't have to, I was done in under an hour. I guess I had less homework this week than last week.

Dr. Phil: I wouldn't think so. I've had lots of kids video their homework and they all bounce on in here the next week with a $#!*-kissing grin and say, "Dr. Phil, I didn't have to watch the video." I think they like throwing it back in my face.

Dale: Yeah, kind of I guess, but I didn't have to. I was done.

Dr. Phil: Great, but why were you done?

Dale: I told you. I think I must'a got less homework this week.

Dr. Phil: Could it be you pressed the tape button and sat right down and did your work. No screwing around? No phone calls? No looking for stuff?

Dale: (mouth open) I guess.

We all get in our own way. What Dale experienced was that if he simply started and got it done, the task seemed to be smaller. He didn't have to carry his own attitude around during the "fighting doing homework process." Less attitude weight, less work.

Think about your last few days. Have you allowed your attitude to get in the way of your goals?

I once met a cool old farmer who made millions in the cow business. He was a whiz with numbers and always good for a dirty joke or two (hundred). He told me that the hard part of being a rancher for him was getting up at 4:45 AM. I asked him how he pulled himself out of bed so early every morning. He said, "My pappy used to tell me, 'Pretend it's something you want to do.'" Attitude counts, even at 4:45 AM.

YOU'RE TIRED

HALF OUR LIFE IS SPENT TRYING TO FIND SOMETHING TO DO WITH THE TIME WE HAVE RUSHED THROUGH LIFE TRYING TO SAVE.

Will Rogers

It's hard to get stuff done when you're tired. I joked earlier about "sleeping fast", but it can't be done. Your brain has to clean itself and do daily maintenance or you lose skills. You cannot be efficient when you're tired.[20] A lot of research has been focused on sleep. If you think about it, the Armed Forces would love to have a soldier who didn't need sleep. The research shows that we lose mental acuity when we are tired. If you go without sleep it is not safe. Tired people get injured. Tired people make mistakes.[21,22]

No one likes to hear this, but pulling all-nighters is a terrible way to do a good job on a quarterly report. Research shows that little is retained in one's long-term memory and anxiety is significantly increased. Lack of sleep lowers your hand eye coordination and overall reflexes accounting for many preventable trips to the emergency room.

Respect yourself, make quality sleep a priority.

LACK OF FOCUS

It seems very simple to most patients in my office that you need to make a choice before you can do something. I am often told, "I have so much to do that I can't get anything accomplished."

Zoë had just turned twenty-six and was working in her first professional job at a midsize law firm. She was feeling the pressure of work when her boyfriend of five years dropped a bombshell on her. He was planning on taking a job four hours away and would only be able to see her on weekends. Her

20- Van Dongen HPA, Maislin G, Mullington JM, Dinges DF. The cumulative cost of additional wakefulness: Dose-response effects on neurobehavioral functions and sleep physiology from chronic sleep restriction and total sleep deprivation. Sleep 2003;26:117-28.
21- Harrison Y, Horne JA. Sleep loss impairs short and novel language tasks having a prefrontal focus. J Sleep Res 1998;7:95-100.
22- Dinges DF, Kribbs NB. Performing while sleepy: effects of experimentally-induced sleepiness. In: Monk TH, ed. Sleep, sleepiness and performance. Chichester: John Wiley & Sons, 1991:97-128.

boss, a supportive and caring man, advised her to come and see me when she yelled at the copy machine and scared the office staff.

Zoë: I am being pulled in a million directions. I can't seem to get anything done.

Dr. Phil: What counts most to you?

Zoë: I don't care about any of it, it's all just $#!* to me!

Dr. Phil: Then why are you bothered?

Zoë: Aren't you listening. I'm going crazy!

Dr. Phil: I doubt it. But you are being emotionally pulled apart. What do you want to do?

Zoë: I don't have any idea (She stared sadly at her shoes).

Dr. Phil: If you don't know what you want to do, you're doing it. Nothing. You've become ineffectual.

Zoë: Can you fix me?

Dr. Phil: You're not broken, you need to focus on what really counts to you. One thing at a time.

Zoë: I can't do that ... I'm swamped at work and I think my boyfriend is dumping me. I don't blame him. I want to dump me too (she half smiled)!

Dr. Phil: I'm not advocating for you to do one thing at a time all day or all week. I want you to focus on one thing at a time throughout your day. When you're at work, focus on the one project that needs your attention the most. When you're at home, focus on the one thing that needs the most attention.

Without focus, Zoë was getting nothing done in any part of her life. When she was at work, she was thinking about home. When she was driving, she was thinking law. When she was with her boyfriend, she was feeling work stress. It's back to the old question: How do you eat an elephant? The answer: One bite at a time. If the bite is too big and it is choking you, you need to spit it out and cut it into smaller bites. You can eat an elephant one bite at a time. And, you can accomplish even difficult tasks one bite at a time. However, even at one bite at a time, you need to focus on what you are doing.

I have listed some of the more common reasons that people choke on their responsibilities. Each tends to give talented people lots of difficulty. By keeping these problem areas in mind, and by cutting them into smaller pieces, you will be able to accomplish your desired goals.

UNDEFINED GOALS

You have to be able to define a task to accomplish it. Force yourself to develop a specific definition of what it is you need to get done. It is easy to be pulled off course if you do not clearly see where you are heading.

Leroy told me that he wanted to pick up extra work doing odd jobs in his neighborhood. I asked him what he would put on a big billboard if he could afford a billboard. After a few minutes he said, "I want to make money!"

Leroy was focusing on his need, he wanted money. But, that wasn't going to get someone in the neighborhood to hire him to clean out his or her gutters. Leroy's problem was that he wanted to make money (a really big bite). He had to spit this problem out and cut it into smaller stuff. With a little practice he came up with the following list, which he made into a flyer (Leroy's charm came through in his flyer and in person).

By the time we've made it, we've had it.

Malcolm Forbes

Honest hard working high school
senior looking for honest hard work

My mom has allowed me lots of experience:

Washing windows
Scrubbing floors, toilets and driveways
Moving furniture and cleaning carpets
Painting inside and out

Dependable

On his handouts he listed his mother as a reference and asked prospective customers to call his mother to confirm his skills.

Leroy made $1800 dollars and was later hired by a neighbor to work the counter at his dry cleaning business. He worked there for the two years he went to junior college.

You need to define your goals so that you can make sure you are focusing on what you value. For example, when I was twenty I worked at McDonald's. It afforded me income with a flexible schedule. I showed up on time and I did what was asked of me. Most of the time I enjoyed my experience, especially when we were busy. Time seemed to whiz by when we were busy.

I knew that I was not planning to learn how to manage a McDonald's and make it my career. For me, McDonald's was not a career move; it was a stepping-stone to help me work my way through college. I also learned a lot. To this day I am impressed with how McDonald's is able to make a few pennies profit per customer add up to billions of dollars of corporate earnings.

I recall getting teased by friends for working at McDonald's. But, as I saw it, I had an honest job that worked into my ever-changing class schedule. My focus was on getting good grades. I was not concerned that I didn't have the most glamorous job.

Once I was assigned to write a paper on how to do something. The English professor wanted a paper that was so clearly written that an average person could do the task just by reading the paper. I wrote about how to make 64 Big Macs at one time. On busy nights, or when a school team bus pulled in, I would whip out 64 Big Macs in minutes.

McDonald's and that English assignment have served me numerous times over the years. I have often been paid for writing a "how to" article. How to talk to your teen about sex. How to defuse anger in the work place. And, I often need to whip out six burgers or four omelets or a large load of ribs at home.

It is important to keep focused on your goals and creatively adjust to get your short and long term needs met.

Jan consulted with me because she was sure she was not ready for her new promotion. Jan, at age twenty-four, had just found out that she was the new Promotions Director for a mid size radio station. She had all the necessary skills and her goal was to capture this job before her twenty-fifth birthday. However, when it happened, she found herself not sleeping.

Jan's concern was that she was unable to keep track of all her business responsibilities. She reported that she spent half her time looking for papers, contracts, or her glasses. After we talked for a bit it was obvious to me that Jan was highly motivated and incredibly skilled. Her biggest problem was that she was easily distracted. Once Jan mastered the following issues, she shined in her new position.

Clutter: Your workspace has to be organized. By keeping necessary things within hand's reach and everything else out of the way, you can help yourself focus. Knickknacks and candy dishes draw your attention away from the task at hand. Most people find that order helps job completion.

Phone: The phone is a tool. Just because it rings, doesn't mean it needs to be answered. Don't let the phone control you. A 30 second phone call can take you off task for a few minutes. It is usually best to stop phone interruptions when you need to focus your mind on a task for a chunk of time.

Interruptions: Control your environment. If your work area is an open door to the world, people will interrupt you and you will be constantly distracted. Protect your space. Control your space (be polite). I was impressed to learn that scary writer, Stephen King, found that his little laundry room with a rickety little school desk worked just fine for him. He liked being tucked off in an obscure place, away from distractions.

You need to control your environment so that you are not distracted. Find what works for you. I did most of my graduate dissertation in the middle of the night at a dumpy restaurant. I found the restaurant noise and the bad coffee helped me block out the world.

Don't get caught up in the look of your quiet space, your control over it is what is important. If you need total quiet, make your workspace quiet. If you need lots of light, sun up the place. Respect your needs—then get focused on task completion.

Pearl (16) told me why she got her final history paper in late.

It was like the whole world was against me. I had only six hours before my paper was due and everything went wrong. I even skipped school to work on it. I couldn't find all my reference notes so I had to go on-line and get them again. That took an hour. My brother used up all the printer ink and I had to go the to store. The traffic was horrible. I couldn't believe it. It cost thirty dollars! I was so pissed. I had to go to my mom's work and get money. She was pissed that I skipped school. She just doesn't understand that I had to skip school so that I could get the damn paper in by the end of school.

I finally got the stupid paper done and I couldn't get the computer to talk to the printer. I just wanted to throw the thing against the wall. It turned out to be the cord thing. I got the thing printed, but I didn't have a folder to put it in. So I had to go back to the store. When I got the whole thing put together, I wanted to glue a picture onto the front cover. I couldn't find any glue in the whole house. I had to go back to the damn store. Three times I had to fight with traffic.

When I finally got it all put together it looked great. I couldn't believe it when my brother came home. School was over. I turned it in the next day and Mr. Johnson didn't even want to believe that I really tried. The best grade I can get on it now is only a 'B'.

Pearl is not unique. I hear this type of story all the time.

If you don't plan, you are doomed. A little planning saves a lot of frustration. How to plan will be covered further when we discuss personal organization skills later in this chapter.

I HAVE REALIZED THAT THE PAST AND FUTURE ARE REAL ILLUSIONS, THAT THEY EXIST IN THE PRESENT, WHICH IS WHAT THERE IS AND ALL THERE IS.

Alan Watts

For want of a nail[23] is a proverb dating back to the 14th century:

> For want of a nail the shoe was lost.
> For want of a shoe the horse was lost.
> For want of a horse the rider was lost.
> For want of a rider the battle was lost.
> For want of a battle the kingdom was lost.
> And all for the want of a horseshoe nail.

Benjamin Franklin wrote a variation of the proverb in the preface of *Poor Richard's Almanac*[24]:

> A little neglect may breed mischief...
> for want of a nail, the shoe was lost;
> for want of a shoe the horse was lost;
> and for want of a horse the rider was lost.

I bet that procrastination is the most common way people hold themselves back. The word comes from its Latin roots (pro) toward (crastination) tomorrow. The problem is that when we procrastinate, tomorrow leads to the next day, which leads to the next day. Days become weeks and before you know it, life passes you by.

Procrastination means: To put off doing something, especially out of habitual carelessness or laziness. Put simply, procrastination is a choice.

A Chinese proverb says, "The best time to plant a tree was twenty years ago. The second best time is now." It may be an old Chinese saying, but it still works for today. A new American saying could be, "The best time to buy milk is before you need it." Not as classy but accurate. So, the next time you're feeling pressure over your stuff ask yourself, "Wouldn't it have felt good to have had this stuff done yesterday?"

Over the years I have asked lots of people about their procrastination. What I learned is that most people put off stuff they don't like. Wow! We don't want to start what we don't like. Yep. We avoid discomfort. This was discussed earlier when I advocated for you to leave your comfort zone to cre-

23- c 1390 Gower Confessio Amantis v. 4785.
24- Benjamin Franklin, Poor Richards Almanack, June 1758, The Complete Poor Richard Almanacks, facsimile ed., vol. 2, pp. 375, 377.

ate the life you want. You have to confront little discomforts to defeat procrastination.

I have a few suggestions about how to stop the cycle of procrastination. First, recognize it. You have to be aware of your tendency towards procrastination to realize that it is controlling you. Once you notice procrastination's retched breath, you will find the following head games helpful:

Do the worst first: When you have tasks that you must do but don't want to, do the worst task first. This makes the process feel easier. It's very hard to keep going if the job gets even worse. It is easier to stay motivated if the job gets a little better. Remember, your perception counts.

Make a game out of it: Find a way to put some fun into the crappy job. Set up a way to play with yourself (hey, clean your mind up and stick with me here!). Time yourself, attack the job sideways, add music. Be creative. Laugh in the face of despair. Joke with the toilet as you clean it. Humor helps us to get through many a $#!*ty task.

For a lot of people, setting a deadline for themselves is a game that brings rewards. "I'll get this done by 4:15 if it kills me!" It is self-talk that is motivating.

Add a reward: Pat yourself on the back for your hard work. If it's a beautiful day and you can't stand that you're stuck inside, reward yourself with a walk around the block after you get half your work done. I know a business tycoon who rewards himself with five minutes of shooting hoops after he completes an undesirable task. Keep the reward simple and low calorie. If you get a candy bar after each undesirable task, you will weigh five hundred pounds in no time. I find that physical activity works well for most people. Walk, hoops, or juggle to help relieve life's tensions. Again, be creative.

Start: Lots of people spend so much time getting ready to start that the project doubles. If Stephen King can make millions of dollars writing in his laundry room, you should be able to kick ass with your cool stuff. I once watched my sister prepare all afternoon for a date that lasted two and a

BEWARE OF THE MAN WHO WORKS HARD TO LEARN SOMETHING, LEARNS IT, AND FINDS HIMSELF NO WISER THAN BEFORE... HE IS FULL OF MURDEROUS RESENTMENT OF PEOPLE WHO ARE IGNORANT WITHOUT HAVING COME BY THEIR IGNORANCE THE HARD WAY.

Kurt Vonnegut
Cat's Cradle

half hours. Four hours of prep for two and a half hours of date. Life's too short. It's like taking off a band-aid, just rip the damn thing off, feel the pain for a moment, then go on with your life. Slowly peeling a band-aid off lets you feel it for minutes versus seconds. As the Nike sneaker ads tell you: Just Do It!

You can never finish a task if you don't ever start. Life rewards action. You have to complete a task to reap rewards.

Total Void: There are areas in our daily lives where we can become totally void of thought. In these Total Void zones we will find ourselves staring off into the ether with little sign of life registering on our faces. When this occurs it is easy to have thirty minutes quickly turn into three hours. In Total Void our mind is being occupied by random thoughts of nothing. Like a black hole in outer space, the Total Void takes thought into it and never lets it escape. It warps time and space while sucking the life out of its victims. No light can escape a black hole, and no time can be retrieved from a Total Void.

There are many types of Total Voids in the known universe. The most common is the TV. I once played with the knob on the side marked brightness but the programming didn't get any smarter. For lots of people the TV is the kiss of death for creativity and the fertilizer in the garden of procrastination. My advice is to be fearful of the TV. It can suck the life out of you. But, at the same time, I like TV. What a conundrum. My advice—plan your viewing. Turn on the TV just before the show you want to watch starts and (this part is hard) turn the dumb thing off the instant the show ends. Karl Marx said, "Religion ... is the opium of the people." To which I say, "TV is the marijuana." You should even beware of "educational" television. Do you really need to watch a show about the mating rituals of the fruit fly at 2:00 AM? Not if you will be tired tomorrow and frustrated that you are behind in something significantly more important to your real life than fly humping (unless you're a horny fruit fly, that is. If so watch on!).

The second Total Void is drugs, with alcohol and pot being the most common avoidance tools. Most people find that drugs and task completion don't go together. I'm told regularly something like, "I work better a little buzzed." My observations of life, along with all the brain research I have studied, disagree with that contention.

A third Total Void is small talk. Lots of people use small talk and gossip to fill their lives versus improving their lives with accomplishments. When I worked at County Mental Health earlier in my career, I was amazed how many people showed up to work at 8:00 AM to visit, drink coffee, fix their makeup, eat a donut, complain about their weight, and gossip about others who were not present. Then around 9:15 they started work. These same individuals were quick to bitch about their hefty workload at every opportunity. I have heard similar stories from numerous types of businesses across America. I would guess that there are billions of dollars in lost productivity in our nation's workplaces because of small talk and coffee.

In the area of Total Void, everyone has to decide for him or herself what is more important to them—life accomplishments or avoiding life. I'm very liberal minded, it's your life… what ya gonna do?

NEED FOR PERFECTION

Many people have a need to do everything at the highest level of accuracy. As a result they are paralyzed when it comes time to get started. If you find your self-talk saying, "There is no way I can get that looking the way it needs to look because…" or "I can't get it that polished in only…" you are destroying your own creative powers.

A good rule of thumb is to do the best you can in the time allotted. I find that people do amazingly well with a 90% goal versus a 100% goal. Ninety percent is still 'A' work, but not perfect. Depending on the task, even 'C' work may be good enough.

If your goal is to be a good athlete, but you are not the one in a million superstar of your sport, then maybe it is more reasonable to be a 'C' athlete who gets good exercise, enjoys companionship, and loves winning at your skill level. The alternative would be not playing tennis because you are naturally a 'C' tennis player. Check your attitude.

Max came to my office because he was having anxi-

PERFECTIONISM IS SIMPLY PUTTING A LIMIT ON YOUR FUTURE. WHEN YOU HAVE AN IDEA OF PERFECT IN YOUR MIND, YOU OPEN THE DOOR TO CONSTANTLY COMPARING WHAT YOU HAVE NOW WITH WHAT YOU WANT. THAT TYPE OF SELF CRITICISM IS SIGNIFICANTLY DETERRING.

John Eliot
Reverse
Psychology for
Success

ety attacks. One day he had trouble breathing and went to the emergency room because he feared a heart attack. After much testing he was assured that he hadn't had a heart attack, but that if he kept up his present level of personal stress, he probably would have a heart attack in his mid forties. Max was twenty-three when I met him. He was working at a full time job and spending the rest of his awake time writing a computer game program. It came down to that he lived on coffee and snack cakes, slept little and pushed himself to the max (sorry about the pun).

As it turned out, Max was close to marketing his game on three occasions in the previous 18 months. Each time he thought he was ready, he read in a computer game magazine that someone else had tweaked their product in some way so that Max felt he had to "better" that tweak in his program. At this rate Max was never going to get his product to market. His need to produce the perfect game meant that his program would never see the glow of a monitor.

Max explained, "This program is my life ... I can't put out a second rate product, it has to be the best."

So, I ask you, would it be better for Max to release a very good program, let's say an 'A-96%' program and later put out version A.1 then A.2, or for Max to keep playing with his mouse like a computerized hamster?

TIME MANAGEMENT AND PERSONAL ORGANIZATION SKILLS

Time management is really personal value management. You need to choose one task over another. Should you do your homework, or should you watch TV? Should you start to go through your stacks of boring receipts for your tax preparer, or should you go on-line and chat up some cyber sex toy?

In fact, it is much more complicated than just one choice. Literally, it is to do one task over every other task on the planet. If you choose to go and feed the homeless, you are choosing not to do everything else. If you choose to sleep in, you choose not to do every other conceivable choice that you could do. You need to manage your time through your personal values.

If a friend asks you to go fishing and you decline because you have to go to work, you are choosing work over fishing. You are placing more value on going to work than you are on going fishing. Your values need to be clear in your own mind. Only when your values are clear within your thoughts can you make choices that are correct for you.

Prior to planning your time, you have to decide what really matters to you. By knowing what you want, you force behaviors upon yourself. For example, are you willing to invest eleven years in higher education to be a nuclear physicist or a medical doctor? Are you willing to devote ten years to the piano to become a concert caliber pianist? In addition to the time, are you capable of being a nuclear physicist, medical doctor, or concert pianist?

HONEST LIMITATIONS

We have all heard it millions of times, "You can do anything you put your mind to." The reason for this type of touchy-feely statement is to encourage individuals not to give up too easily. At the dojo I workout at, one of the Black Belts likes to spout that very saying. "You can do anything you put your mind to." One day I privately pointed out that the saying was hollow even if he meant well. He backed his belief with all his heart.

"I tell the kids that they can make it, that they are great and that I believe in them. They just have to believe in themselves!"

"I think I can prove you wrong." I smiled.

"You just don't believe in the kids like I do!"

"I believe in you, please hold your breath for ten minutes."

Just because you want something doesn't mean that it will happen. What you have to watch out for is quitting on yourself before you have really investigated all the options.

When I was starting junior high school many of my friends were enthusiastic about becoming astronauts. The American space program was getting lots of attention and my friends were looking towards the heavens with hopeful eyes. One particular lunch period I became the butt of jokes because I an-

I FIND TELEVISION VERY EDUCATING. EVERY TIME SOMEBODY TURNS ON THE SET, I GO INTO THE OTHER ROOM AND READ A BOOK.

Groucho Marx

nounced that I had no desire to go to work at NASA. I was afraid of heights and space seemed pretty high off the ground to me. (I still don't want to be an astronaut, but I wouldn't mind a Star Trek type space shuttle to buzz around in.) I bring this up because part of knowing yourself is knowing your limitations. My fear of heights has also limited my desire to be an elevator repairman, a balloonist, or a window washer. If you are five foot one in all directions, your pro basketball career looks doomed. But your love of basketball could lead you to the broadcast booth or to write for a sports magazine. More on this later.

Your personal values set the stage for your activities. If it is your belief that life is short and to be cherished, you won't waste time well. If you believe that life is cheap and everlasting, what you do with any particular moment or afternoon doesn't matter much to you.

PREDICTING TIME

Once I was driving with my family over the bridge into the San Francisco Bay area. When I got to the toll both area there was a commotion. My family and I were driving in the free direction. Motorists in the other direction had to stop and pay a toll. From what I could tell, a car was sideways and smashed into the protective barrier in front of the toll both. Another car was smashed into the first car. Then another car, and another. It looked like eight or ten cars were trying to share the exact same space. Many cars were now stopping. As I continued onto the bridge I could see miles and miles of cars that were soon to be stuck due to the accident ahead of them. I turned back to my sons and said, "I can predict the future of those drivers."

"What?" One son questioned.

"You and I know more about their lives than they do. We know that in a minute or so they are going to be in a huge traffic jam."

At that moment, off in the distance, my son pointed out a small red flashing vehicle. A little later we passed an emergency vehicle as it went towards the accident. The emergency vehicle was moving all of twenty miles an hour along the shoulder of the road. In no time the traffic jam was miles long.

When we got to San Jose, two hours later, KGO radio was still talking about the terrible traffic mess caused by the drunk driver who hit the tollbooth.

This story illustrates that it is possible, in certain circumstances, to be able to predict the future. I know that, if all goes well at 7:00 o'clock this evening, I will pick up son #1 at soccer practice and at 7:15 I will pick up son #2 at the dojo. How do I know that? I know it because this plan is written in my schedule for today. It states:

3:00 PM	Work on Thought Mines: Time management
7:00 PM	Pick up Ethan @ Soccer
7:15 PM	Pick up Josh @ Jujitsu.

If all goes well, at 6:45 I will be closing down the computer and heading for the car. Soccer is 10 minutes away from my office. At 7:00 I should be picking up a sweaty, red faced teenager... and so on.

I know all this because I keep a day planner. Nothing fancy, but it is very important for my life's organization. I have kept one since high school. I have a few simple rules for planning my days, and as long as I don't break my own rules I tend to get lots done with a minimum of personal grief.

"Stop, wait a minute!" you might be saying, "A daily planner? Isn't that for busy executives? I'm not a rich businessman with lots to do. I'm not the kind of person who needs a fancy day planner, PDA, or a Blackberry."

You may not be a rich executive, but you are busy. You do have a life. You do have things to plan.

Don't let the day planner throw you. What I want to discuss with you is a tool to help you get your needs met. It is personal. It is about you and your needs.

If you knew that at seven tonight you were going to be in a huge traffic jam, on a bridge, in earthquake country, would you try to avoid the situation? Well, in a personal way, my daily calendar focuses me on what I want to accomplish and how important, to me, each task is. I try to use my 86,400 seconds to the fullest. I work hard and I play hard. What I don't do is worry hard. I have noticed however, that people do a lot of worrying about forgetting things.

IF HISTORY REPEATS ITSELF, AND THE UNEXPECTED ALWAYS HAPPENS, HOW INCAPABLE MUST MAN BE OF LEARNING FROM EXPERIENCE.

George Bernard Shaw

I think of planning in the same way cows eat. When a cow chows down on some sweet clover, she chomps away and fills up one of her four stomachs. Then, later on, she goes and hangs out over there and chews her cud. What she is doing is bringing up lunch and re-chewing the really fibrous stuff again, and maybe again. This sounds nasty (and it is), but for the cow it is the best way to get all the nutrition out of her fibrous diet. In cow speak this is called rumination, the act of chewing cud.

Lots of people also ruminate. They bring up stuff all day and make sure that they keep it on their mind. Some people worry all day and all night long. So, if you have a meeting at say 4:00, you keep it on your mind throughout your entire day. You think of it at 1:15. You ruminate at 2:37 and again at 3:11. Now that takes a lot of brainpower. In fact, I contend it takes a lot of wasted brainpower.

Virgil was very upset. He was angry with himself for forgetting an appointment.

Virgil: Yesterday I was supposed to go and put in an application for a new job. I talked to the manager last week and he said he would be happy to talk to me. I politely asked him to commit to a time. I was all excited about the interview. I just simply forgot.

Dr. Phil: You forgot?

Virgil: Yeah. I was thinking about it all week. I was looking forward to the interview. At about six last night it dawned on me that I forgot.

Dr. Phil: You didn't forget. You remembered at six. You remembered at the wrong time.

Virgil: I hadn't thought about it like that. I guess I didn't really forget.

Virgil was blaming his memory. But in fact, it was not his memory that was faulty. It was the tool he used to trigger his memory.

Virgil: At around three I went off with friends to hang. I wasn't doing anything.

Dr. Phil: You were doing something. You were hanging out with your friends.

What Virgil needed was a plan. He thought he had one, but it proved not to work very well for him. So now he needs a better plan. He needs to have some way for him to trigger his own memory so that he can do a particular behavior, like go to the job interview, at a particular time.

Repetitive worry is a poor tool for keeping organized. We tend to be able to ruminate only when we are not involved with some meaningful act, like during math class, or a boring meal, or when we should be sleeping. When we are with friends, all involved with the entertainment value of the interaction, time goes by. The more involved we are the quicker time goes by. Thus, at six o'clock Virgil brought back up his cud and started chewing. Then he remembered, 4:00 Interview. You snooze you lose, the saying goes. Unfortunately, when Virgil called to try to set up another interview, the manager didn't return his calls.

EXCUSES/LIES

Over the years I have noticed that most people react to their life, versus controlling their life. If you do not plan your days you will be dealing with stuff as it occurs, you will need to be reactive. If you plan your day you have large portions of time during which you are in control. Not every minute, but lots of minutes. You will be proactive. You will be choosing your path. This is important to me. I hate to be told what to do. I like to tell myself what to do. Whenever possible I want to be proactive. If I had been stuck on the other side of the highway in the earlier story, I would have had little choice but to be stuck in a traffic jam. I couldn't wish the auto accident away. But, I could have had proactive choices about how I reacted to the sudden change in my plans, a change that I had little to do with. I might have chosen to visit with my family, but after hours in the car, well, we would probably be all visited out. I might have tried to find an impromptu card game or read or checked through mail or written a letter. I know that I cannot always control my life, so I actually plan for inconvenience. When we travel, I bring reading materials, cards, a chess game, paper and pens. I take reading material that is important to me when I

EVERY COMPOSER KNOWS THE ANGUISH AND DESPAIR OCCASIONED BY FORGETTING IDEAS WHICH ONE HAD NO TIME TO WRITE DOWN.

Hector Berlioz

Philip Copitch, Ph.D. 117

go to the doctor's office so I am not stuck reading whatever I can find. I have often joked to friends, "As soon as I am stuck somewhere, I'm going to..." What I am really saying is, that at this moment I am too busy to do whatever it is right now, but I would like to. So, when some unscheduled time drops in my lap, I'm going to. Over the years I have noticed that people have lots of excuses for not planning their day. I politely call them excuses, but really I think of them as personal lies. Let's look at some of the biggies.

I'M TOO BUSY TO PLAN

This is the most common excuse. "Who has time to do that every day?" The answer: People who wish to get stuff done! If you won $86,400 dollars would you spend fifteen minutes planning what you were going to do with it? I surely would, in fact a lot longer. And, I would enjoy playing with the thoughts of what I could do with the money.

Well, you have 86,400 seconds tomorrow, what are you going to do with them? At this point you might be thinking, a second is very small. Who cares! You're right, but what second are you thinking about? If you hold your breath for ten seconds, no big whoop. But, after two minutes every second is really noticeable. I suspect that each second you hold your breath you will get more respect for the "insignificant" second. If you have no plan for yourself tomorrow, you are giving yourself permission to be reactive every second of the day.

A daily plan puts you in control of your time. Your time is a valuable commodity that you cannot replace.

I HATE NOT BEING FREE, A DAILY PLANNER IS CONTROLLING

A daily planner is controlling, self-controlling. You are indeed responsible for controlling yourself.

My daily planner is my behavioral map to success. As I have told you before, I am basically lazy. If I didn't control my basic desire to butt hug my couch and watch TV, I would be the best couch potato on planet Earth. In my daily planner I plan work, play, and do nothing time. When I am following my plan I

LAWYERS SPEND A GREAT DEAL OF THEIR TIME SHOVELING SMOKE.

Oliver Wendell Holmes Jr.

EVERYWHERE IS WALKING DISTANCE IF YOU HAVE THE TIME.

Steven Wright

am not feeling guilty because I know that I planned my day according to my values. I plan based on what I believe is correct for me. I plan towards my own personal definition of success. I guarantee I will not pass judgment on how you define your personal success as long as you are not hurting other people and you are feeling creative. It is your life. Create with it.

MY LIFE IS BORING, I HAVE NOTHING TO PLAN

Everyone has a routine life. Often this can feel boring. But it is not routine or boring—it is life. If you're bored, you are boring. Why would you want to be boring? Spice up your life.

George hated his Monday through Friday mornings. He was a high school senior and ready to go to college, but he still had months to go before he was a high school graduate. His grades were good and he was already accepted for college. He was treading water. A week after we talked he told me that he had found a book of seldom-used words. He had been carrying it with him in has backpack. When he found that he had a few wasted minutes he would flip open the book and try to learn one new word. He started asking his friends what they thought the word meant and it had led to a game. One teacher even asked him where he got the book (garage sale, 25¢). George was playing mind candy. Something small and sweet to make something out of nothing. Earth shattering? No. But a valuable use of time for a man who wants to be a sports writer.

PLANNING DOESN'T WORK FOR ME, I ALREADY TRIED IT ONCE

My Uncle Joe once told me, "If you fish in the desert you won't snag your line, but you won't find fish either." Uncle Joe was a strange old bird, but what I think he was teaching me is that a bad plan is just as bad as no plan.

It takes a little bit of practice to find a system that works for you. There are lots of planners sold in office supply stores that seem to be an OK starting place. But, what I found was that they did not work for me. They were designed to work well for everybody, but I am just a single body. So over the years I begged, borrowed, and stole the best of lots of planners and simplified all of these into one that works well for me. I do mean simplified. Most of the "systems" I have seen are a six week course within themselves to get me to fit into their planner. That is not my style. I like my world more simple, less flash (remember, I am basically lazy.)

Over the next few pages I will explain one simple way that lots of people have found useful. I advise that you try it for a day or two, then play with it and make it yours. It isn't fancy, but it is functional. This little planner has made me lots of money too. I have used it for years to organize my world.

As I said earlier, my daily planner is my behavioral map to success, success in the broadest sense of the word.

DR. PHIL'S TWO SHEET SIMPLE PLANNER

My planner consists of two pages of 8 1/2 by 11 inch copy paper. Page one has the hours of the day and check boxes followed by a short line for small tasks. I have one full week at a time on that page (some people like planners that are laid out one page per day which gives them lots of little chunks of time). Page two is full of lots of lines and wide-open space to jot notes and thoughts down. That's it. I guess it uses about 5¢ worth of paper. I made mine up on a computer and copy it over and over onto 3 hole-punched paper. I keep it stored in a three ring binder. Originally it was a plastic one, but now I have a cool leather binder I received as a birthday present (20 birthdays ago). I write the dates in by hand and double check that I am doing it correctly. I keep three months of calendar paper in my binder at a time. I choose not to plan out past about a month. Far away plans like weddings or vacations I keep on a monthly calendar in the back of the binder. Pretty simple. Let's look at each part and how it works.

Figure 4: Section A and Section B: Daily Calendar and Do List

SECTION A: HOURS OF THE DAY - THE CHUNKS

When I commit to doing something that is time related I write it down, in pencil, on the correct line (I do mean "correct" line. If you are not careful, you will show up at the wrong time. Embarrassing, done it!). I write it in pencil because things change. If need be I can move things around.

If you and I commit to getting together at say, 3:00 PM Thursday, May 27, I would go to that day in my planner and write it in. I print so that I can read it on May 27th. I may also jot a short note to myself to jog my memory.

3:00 PM Loyal Reader / talk about planner

This does two important things for me. It lets me forget about Loyal Reader until May 27th, and it will jog my memory about our last conversation. This is important. If I have to keep track of everything in my mind, I will end up completely stressed out. Also, I will never really be able to focus on what I am doing in the present. As we will discuss later, this lack of focus dooms most people to being mediocre.

I have a huge Must Rule, I do not commit to anything without my planner. I keep my planner close by—but safe. If I'm in the dojo getting my butt kicked, my planner is in my car. If I'm at work, my planner is at work. If I'm at home, my planner is

I THINK THAT SOMEHOW, WE LEARN WHO WE REALLY ARE AND THEN LIVE WITH THAT DECISION.

Eleanor Roosevelt

at home. My planner is an extension of my frontal lobe. It is part of my brain matter. If I lose my planner, I am fishing in the desert; I'm royally screwed.

I also write projects in my planner. Such as:

Jujitsu
Lunch with Geri
Pick up Josh
Write report / Smith, A

I schedule my life. I write specifically what I will be doing and when. If I just said to myself, "I need to get some exercise later today", I would just keep putting it off all day (I'm still basically lazy!). I would justify my way out of doing it. But, when I have a planned meeting with myself, I do it. So I set a specific plan and write it in my planner, "3:00 Jujitsu." Then I go do it. It is in my plan, the one I set for myself, based on my personal values. I am in control of my life whenever possible.

If I put on my "Do List": Write report / Smith, A. I now have to find a time slot when I should do it. If it is only on my mind's worry list it is very easy to keep putting it off (the "Do List," Section B, will be discussed on the next page).

I plan things that count: meetings, quiet time, drive time, and naps. If I think I should do it, I plan it. I also plan obligations, responsibilities and wishes. Every month I plan, "Write Checks", a task I detest, but I don't want to forget to pay the electric bill. In my business I pay my bills around the 25th day of the month. I will know which day, because every night I review my upcoming days. I plan which day I will tackle the bills, either the 23rd, 24th, 25th, or 26th, depending on other obligations in the flow of the business month. On a few occasions I have, unfortunately, had to do it at midnight on the 26th. Not my first choice, but for that particular month it was my best choice.

You may have noticed that my day starts at 10:00 AM and ends at 10:00 PM. Remember this is my planner. It is customized for me. I find that I'm stupid before 10:00 AM so I avoid pre-ten as much as possible. Your calendar should reflect your life. I have a friend who loves 5:00 AM. He tells me, "It's quiet, I get my best work done when I'm fresh." I have no idea how he does it. There is only one five on my clock.

You make your daily planner fit your life-style and make sure you can get your sleep.

SECTION B: SMALL ITEM CHECK BOXES.

On page one, next to the hours of the day, I keep my Small Item Check Box List. Most people call it a "To Do List." I tend to think of it as a "Do List." I like to be proactive; I get things done (self-talk slipping out a bit there).

I put things on the Small Item Check Box List page that tend to take less than ten minutes, or bigger things needing to be assigned a time slot.

For example, I may have three phone calls that I would like to make. Each might take five minutes. If I did them all at once, I would need at least fifteen minutes to get all three done. Or, as it may turn out, the people aren't by their phones so I get nothing done in fifteen minutes.

What I do is keep my small stuff handy. When a chunk of time opens up, I grab one of these little projects and I get it done. So, if my five o'clock appointment is late by ten minutes, I'll use the 600 seconds given back to me. I leverage my time. This leveraged time adds up to hundreds of hours every year (it feels like found time, but we know that we only get 86,400 seconds per day).

Instead of staring out of the window, or feeling rejected by the late arrival, I use the time to complete a small task. Throughout my week I will leverage time to:

LIFE IS WHAT HAPPENS TO YOU WHILE YOU'RE BUSY MAKING OTHER PLANS.

John Lennon

· Open junk mail (I like it)
· Make a quick call
· Read short articles
· Read part of a longer article
· Write a thank you note (I have a lot to be thankful for, so I write lots of thank you notes.)
· Pick up messages
· Stretch my lower back (I'm getting old)
· And, my favorite, pee!

This type of "small stuff" takes up a lot of time.

Philip Copitch, Ph.D. 123

So, I use my time wisely. If I'm waiting my turn at the doctor's office, I have a book to read. If I'm stuck—I get little things done. I plan for it, life is inconvenient, and so I can find lots of leverage seconds floating throughout my week.

Figure 5: Section C - Dr. Phil's Big Stuff

SECTION C: THE BIG STUFF

   The page I call the Big Stuff is for big stuff that I want to do, but I can't or don't want to assign a specific time for doing it. If I get an idea, hear an interesting saying, or think of a 'wish I could', I jot it down on this page. Most of the stories and sayings in this book started life on the Big Stuff page. Stuff stays on this page until I find a better home for it.
   For example: the cartoon at the beginning of Chapter 4 started out as a punch line that I hastily wrote down during a meeting. The presenter was very boring and my mind wandered. It tripped over the punch line somewhere during its wanderings and I wrote it down. A few days later, as I was planning my day, I went down the battered page of Big Stuff and made sure that I had found homes for all the stuff that had ended up on it. The last thing I did was to cut out the punch line. Then, I threw the rest of the page away, and dropped the punch line into a red plastic box in my den. The red plastic box is the repository for all potential cartoons.

There it sat for months.

One day, months later, I was on the phone with an insurance company. I was trying to get them to pay for therapy for a kid who needed it. I got placed on hold. While listening to the 'on hold music' I checked out my red fun basket. As I read over the first few notes I wondered how I ever thought that they were funny. I tossed them into the trash. Then I found the punch line "Even if I get Alzheimer's, I'll remember what you just said!" and played with it in my head. Out of leveraged "phone hell" time I found a usable cartoon. Sure beats just listening to the phone-hold band.

You may have noticed the two boxes per line on the Dr. Phil's Do List. The small one is the traditional check box for when the task is done. The larger box is for a prioritizing number. Sometimes I want to prioritize parts of the list to help me easily keep track of what needs to be moved to today's or tomorrow's do list.

The Big Stuff page tends to be the repository of stuff I have hope in. My page today has these four time consuming listings:

Birthday present for Geri
Find garage floor
Drop dead trees
Call Barbara about meeting

These are not tasks—these are part time jobs. But I still need/want to do them. In three weeks my bride is going to have another birthday. After an eternity together, what do you get the woman who has everything and always says, "I don't need anything but time with my family." Or, "Whenever I suggest what I want for my birthday you always say, 'That's not a real present, just go get that yourself!'" Finding a cool present is going to be difficult.

The garage is a nuclear waste site without the radiation. Organizing it is at least an eight-hour job. I haven't had eight free hours to "waste" on a garage in ???? Actually, never have, but I would like it cleaned up.

I have twenty dead or dying trees just off the driveway. Pine Beetle I am told. This is probably a forty-hour job that needs to be done. I need to dry out the trees by sawing them up to interrupt the

EVERYTHING SHOULD BE MADE AS SIMPLE AS POSSIBLE, BUT NOT ONE BIT SIMPLER.

Albert Einstein

I WRITE DOWN EVERYTHING I WANT TO REMEMBER. THAT WAY, INSTEAD OF SPENDING A LOT OF TIME TRYING TO REMEMBER WHAT IT IS I WROTE DOWN, I SPEND THE TIME LOOKING FOR THE PAPER I WROTE IT DOWN ON.

Beryl Pfizer

two-year life cycle of the little beasties.

My job will be to break these tasks down into manageable parts and take on each part. Please notice none of these big jobs are "work" related. These are life related tasks. I don't just plan my workday (or school day), I plan my life. That way I get stuff done.

Another thing on my Big Stuff list was Call Barbara about time of the Red Cross meeting. This ended up there when Barbara called and left a message asking about the meeting. I put the note next to a check box and forgot about it. I was really busy when I got the message, so I put the message in a safe place.

At the end of my day I will take ten minutes to plan for tomorrow. I will check down the lists and move stuff that needs to be moved. Tonight Barbara will go from the big stuff and notes list to the small stuff today list. Tomorrow, during leveraged time, I will call Barbara and tell her the time of the meeting. (Interesting note: Barbara and I were both in the room when the Red Cross meeting was scheduled. I wrote it down and forgot it. Barbara planned on remembering it, but now isn't sure and called me. Sweet lady but disorganized.)

WHAT ELSE IS IN THE PLANNER BINDER?

- I keep a pencil
- My phone book (Printout from my computer. Updated whenever I remember to do it. Usually twice a year.)
- Plain paper
- Up to twenty pieces of paper to read. An article cut out of a magazine, a letter with a map I will need next week, and jokes or articles people give me. This is for leveraging time if I'm stuck away from my normal haunts (waiting for kids after school, waiting for a meeting to start). I've leveraged time at all sorts of places. Movie theaters, baseball games, waiting for a friend in the hospital to wake up and visit with me. One kid called me an intellectual Boy Scout. I guess I am.

WHAT TO AVOID:

I suggest you avoid sticky notes, scraps of paper, the backs of envelopes, or writing on yourself. All these types of notes tend to get lost or washed off or build on themselves. Sticky pads were a great money-maker for 3M, but do not really help people stay organized.

TEN MINUTE PLANNING TIME EVERY DAY

If you use the simple two-page planner described above, you will find that you get lots more done. Once you become clearly aware of what you wish to accomplish today, you have a better chance of getting it done.

Probably the best thing the simple two-page planner does for people is it relieves worry. Worry? Yes worry. Many people spend lots of time worrying about forgetting stuff or getting stuff done. Lots of people have a hard time going to sleep at night because they play their next day over and over in their minds, hoping not to screw something up. This is emotionally draining and dysfunctional.

For example: If I want to call Bob tomorrow, I write it on my Small Item do list and don't think about it until my next planning time. My planning time is the last ten minutes of my "work" day. At the end of my day, whenever that is, I open my planner and look over tomorrow. I read down Section A and make sure that I understand what I expect out of myself. I double-check things like drive time or location. If I have a 3:00 at my office, I make sure that I can be at my office before 3:00. If I have to be across town, I make sure I have the "drive time" calculated correctly so I can be on time. I double-check that I have what I need for my set appointments.

Next, I look down my Section B. I appoint larger items to open time slots. So, if I have a report to read for my 3:00 meeting, I appoint 30 minutes to read the report at 11:00. I move the item from my Do List to a time slot. It is now an appointment. I have an appointment with a stack of paper. With experience I have learned about how long it takes me to read a page, so I allot my time accordingly. If tomorrow at 10:50 a friend calls and invites me

IN THE ABSENCE OF CLEARLY-DEFINED GOALS, WE BECOME STRANGELY LOYAL TO PERFORMING DAILY TRIVIA UNTIL ULTIMATELY WE BECOME ENSLAVED BY IT.

Robert Heinlein

to coffee, I will check my calendar and politely decline, "I have an appointment at 11:00. I can't get away right now." At 3:00 when I attend my meeting I will be a lot happier with myself because I read the report, rather than had a cup of coffee with a friend. At 10:50 I may have wanted to go for coffee, but I attended the appointment that I made with myself to prepare for my 3:00.

I never explain why I can't sneak off for coffee. I simply state the fact, "I have an appointment." No guilt involved. I am not disrespecting my friend, I am staying focused. I have an appointment. When I hear people explain themselves it makes me think of them as weak-minded.

"I'd love to go for coffee with you, but I can't. I have to read a report for my 3:00 today. I'm sorry."

I've even heard people try to talk their friends out of doing what they should do.

"AAAH, come on! You can glance over the report later on. It'll only take a few minutes. I really want to have coffee with you!"

This seems selfish to me. His want for coffee is more important than your want to accomplish your task. True friends don't sabotage your goals, they advocate and support them.

Some people like to start their day with a planning session. They start off fresh and they organize their day. I advocate that you plan at the end of your day. That way you don't need to worry about tomorrow because it is all planned. However, if you are really a morning person, it makes sense to do your planning then. The most important part of the ten-minute planning session is that you truly focus on what you want to get done. For those ten minutes you are 100% focused on the task of prioritizing your day.

APPOINTING BIG PROJECTS

Let's look at some real life examples of appointing the parts of a big project. First we will take on a term paper then we will vanquish the garage from hell.

BIG PROJECT EXAMPLE ONE: A TERM PAPER

Big projects often cover days or even months. Lots, if not most people, find big projects overwhelming. For some this feeling is so powerful that it immobilizes them and keeps them from achieving their life goals.

In the real world, big or bigger projects have to be dealt with. They cannot be avoided. They need special care. I advise you to deal with big projects backwards.

Let's use an example of a term paper (It could be any big project like planning a wedding, organizing a school fund-raiser, or developing your career). This term paper is a big deal, 50% of your grade. Today is April 9th and it is due April 30th. You have known about the paper all semester, but finally, today, the instructor defined the parameters of the damn thing. So you turn to April 30/2:00 PM and write: Hand in Term Paper, Psychology 310.

For most people this makes their chest tight. Lots of thoughts cross their minds. Some think, "I've got lots of time, I'll worry about it next week." Others think, "I only have a few weeks, I'll never get this done, why did I sign up for this damn class!" An organized mind thinks, "Another task… lots of parts. How am I going to break this task down so I can easily conquer this term paper?"

A big project can feel like an elephant was shoved down your throat. A big project can feel like it is going to choke you.

So, how do you eat an elephant?

One bite at a time. If when you put that piece into your mouth it is still too big, and it's choking you, you spit it out and cut it up some more. The trick (or art) to dealing with big projects is to make them into lots of small projects. Once they are small ones, you organize dealing with them backwards. Read on, it will become clearer in a few minutes.

Your assignment is to write a term paper on how children learn. It kind of sounds interesting, but you don't know squat about how kids learn. Your first thought is "…they go to school." But, unfortunately, that isn't much of a term paper. I'm going to take you through the process. We are not going to actually set up the term paper we are only going to look at the process. (This book isn't the place for a How To on term papers. If you need information on how to write one however, go to my web site, www. CopitchInc.com, and look under Recommended Links. You will find lots of helpful information for elementary, high school and college students stuck with study problems.)

What you will need is your date book, a pencil, and a monthly calendar with squares for every day.

The facts—
Today's date is: April 9th
The report is due: April 30th
You have 22 days to learn about and write a great report (1,900,800 seconds).

THE REASON MOST PEOPLE NEVER REACH THEIR GOALS IS THAT THEY DON'T DEFINE THEM, OR EVER SERIOUSLY CONSIDER THEM AS BELIEVABLE OR ACHIEVABLE. WINNERS CAN TELL YOU WHERE THEY ARE GOING, WHAT THEY PLAN TO DO ALONG THE WAY, AND WHO WILL BE SHARING THE ADVENTURE WITH THEM.

Denis Watley

Before this report was assigned, you had a pretty full life already. It is going to take some organization skills to use your time to its fullest and get this report done on time.

What do you have to do to write a great report, and how long will each part take? When it comes to the project time be realistic, not hopeful. If you schedule too much time, great—you're done with time left to do something else. But, if you schedule too little time, you're screwed! You can't make more so you will be stressed.

Parts of the Big Project:	Estimated Time
Research the subject	(8.00 hours)
Organize research into outline	(3.00 hours)
Expand on outline into paragraph form	(4.00 hours)
Type first draft of report	(4.00 hours)
Give draft to proofreader	(0.25 hours)
Pick up draft from proofreader	(0.25 hours)
Make changes to draft	(1.00 hours)
Research to fill gaps in paper (polish)	(2.00 hours)
Type changes and further polish	(2.00 hours)
Give second draft to proofreader	(0.25 hours)
Pick up second draft from proofreader	(0.25 hours)
Make final changes, put project to bed	(1.00 hours)
Print out final paper	(0.50 hours)
Total:	26.50 hours

It will take you 26.50 hours to do a great job on this report. The next question is when?

April

Sunday	Monday	Tuesday	Wednesday	Thursday	Friday	Saturday
		1	2	3	4	5
6	7	8	9	10	11	12
13	14	15	16	17	18	19
20	21	22	23	24	25	26
27	28	29	30	1	2	3

Figure 6: Your working calendar

ORGANIZING BIG PROJECTS BACKWARDS IN SMALL CHUNKS ON A MONTHLY CALENDAR

I recommend that we organize your big project time backwards. We start with April 30th. In the square for April 30th write, Hand in Term Paper, Psychology 310, 2:00 PM. Your monthly calendar now is in sync with your daily planner (Hand in Term Paper, Psychology 310, is written in the 2:00 time slot).

Before we go any further, what big events are scheduled in your life from April 9th to April 30th? On the 28th you are planning to go to Sally and Tom's wedding. That day is shot for studying, but the wedding should be fun. Write Sally and Tom's Wedding in the April 28th square. In fact, while you're at it, you need to write, Buy present for Sally and Tom, on your daily planner. You can't go to the wedding empty handed.

Back to April 30th. What would be the very last thing you would need to do before you could Hand in Term Paper, Psychology 310, 2:00 PM? Think small chunks.

You need to print the completed paper out of

the computer. When would you like to do that? Don't say April 29th at 11:59 PM. That is cutting it too close. That is stress inducing. That could put you in a terrible spot. What if at 11:59 PM on April 29th your printer dies, or the electricity goes out, or you have the trudging trots from the cheap food at Sally and Tom's wedding? $#@* happens. Murphy's Law says: What can go wrong will go wrong and usually at the worst possible time. The worst possible time for this term paper would be 11:59 PM on April 29th.

You don't need that aggravation. Planning is supposed to make your life less stressful. Wouldn't it be a lot less stressful if on Saturday, April 27th, you printed out the paper? Assuming all goes well, you're three days ahead of schedule. I guarantee that is stress lowering. Also, when you're at the wedding, you can relax and have a great time. If the paper isn't done, you may find yourself stressing over it and not focusing on fun.

On Saturday, April 27th, write: Print out finished paper. In parentheses put in the time it will take you to get this done: 30 minutes.

Now you take all the parts from above and place them into your monthly calendar. Keep in mind your nature and your other commitments. For example, if you work long hours on Wednesdays, it would be unrealistic to come home and throw yourself into a valuable term paper. Also, be realistic on how much you can really do on one project at a time. Most people can really focus for about four hours. So, if you plan on doing eight or twelve hours of work one day, you'll probably only get four powerful hours out of your brain.

In the appropriate squares write the following:

April 27:	Pick up second draft from proofreader	(0.25 hours)
	Make final changes, put project to bed	(1.00 hours)
	Print out final paper	(0.50 hours)
April 26:	Give second draft to proofreader	(0.25 hours)
April 25:	Research to fill gaps in paper (polish)	(2.00 hours)
	Type changes and further polish	(2.00 hours)
April 23:	Pick up draft from proofreader	(0.25 hours)
	Make changes to draft	(1.00 hours)
April 21:	Give draft to proofreader	(0.25 hours)

April 20:	Type first draft of report	(4.00 hours)
April 18:	Expand on outline into paragraph form	(4.00 hours)
April 14:	Organize research into outline	(3.00 hours)
April 13:	Research the subject	(4.00 hours)
April 11:	Research the subject	(4.00 hours)

Once this is done and it looks realistic for you and your skills, appoint it into your daily planner. Now you're acting organized.

LET'S LOOK AT A FEW STICKY PLACES IN THE BIG PROJECT ORGANIZATION:

Make sure you understand that rewrite is a major part of writing. Do not plan on your report flowing easily from your mind to paper. Writing is work. A common statement between writers is, "I sat at my computer and slit my wrists!" You will have to re-write, and for most people the rewrite is as hard and time consuming as the first writing.

You will need to have a competent proofreader or two. You wrote what is on the paper, so when you try to proof your own work, you know what is supposed to be written. Often you will read what you meant to write, missing the little mistakes. If you have to be your own proofreader, put your paper down for at least a day. This will give your mind a chance to really read what you have on the page. If you read your own work out loud slowly, you have a better chance of catching errors.

Before you give your work to the proofreader, make sure it is ready. Your proofreader is not supposed to fix your shoddy paper, she is supposed to be "a set of new eyes" to catch mistakes.

You need to respect your proofreader. You cannot expect your proofreader to drop everything to proof your work. It is usually best to set an appointment to have your work proofed. If your proofreader states that she can do it, "Wednesday night", it is your job to have it to her before she is ready for it. This takes some planning and coordination. Often college students trade off proofing each others papers. You need to appoint when she will have the proofed paper returned. Your project will come to a halt if the proofreader can't get to your paper. It is crucial to have a good working relationship with your proofreader.

> WE FIND NO REAL SATISFACTION OR HAPPINESS IN LIFE WITHOUT OBSTACLES TO CONQUER AND GOALS TO ACHIEVE.
>
> Maxwell Maltz

One last thing about working with your proof-reader. Don't take their advice personally. If your paper comes back with lots of red marks, it is not a character attack on you. It is the normal process of rewrite. It is much better to fix the mistakes than to turn them in and get a lower grade. A good proofreader is hard to find, so when you find one, treat her like a trusted advisor.

SOMETIMES LIFE GETS IN THE WAY.

What if you are down with the flu on April 25th? You have no choice but to rework your schedule. It is usually pretty easy to rework your schedule if you have planned it well from the get go. The rule of thumb is to try not to move stuff around too much to fix a problem. In your present schedule you have 1.5 hours of work to do on April 25th. You need to find that time somewhere before April 26th at 6:00 PM when you are scheduled to give the paper to the proofreader. If you have to bump the proofreader's time back, you are looking for trouble. What if the proofreader can't get to your paper in a timely fashion?

Sometimes you have a block of time open up. Let's say Friday, April 19th, your date falls through. You now have all evening to fill. You find that you're kind of in a funk. It would be easy to watch TV all night and snack on junk food. But, what if you used this free time to get ahead? You could start on the April 20th work. It will get your mind off your lacking love life and fill you with feelings of accomplishment. OK, it may not be all that, but you won't have anything to show for watching TV all evening (except a few more ounces on your butt), so taking control may actually feel good. It is a way of getting more time. Your cancelled date is found time. Also, if you are done with April 20th's work, you can plan something else (no, not TV) or start working on April 21st's part of the project. You should not give yourself permission to not do your assigned work, but it feels good to be ahead of the project. And, if you get the flu, you won't be too screwed up (Murphy's Law demands the flu on real busy and project vital days).

It takes time to know how long stuff will take to do. You have to be open to learning as you go. You start off using guesstimation to put a project together. Then, with experience, you will learn more about yourself. Some people find that two hours is the most brainpower they can give at one sitting. So this person will need to schedule two sessions at the library, maybe on the same day, with a lunch, or a class in between. Know thyself and don't work against your own abilities.

BIG PROJECT EXAMPLE TWO: TAKING BACK THE GARAGE!

(Hear the horror music)

What you will need is your date book, a pencil, and a monthly calendar with squares for every day. When you read through how to organize a term paper you had someone outside of yourself determining when you would turn it in. As my friend Irene would say it, "You had a drop-dead date." Irene ran a large printing enterprise and regularly had to juggle hundreds of high dollar deadlines. Even though she was a woman in her sixties, see seemed to get energized as the day went on. Irene used the concept of "drop-dead" to keep the fear of failure at bay. I heard her say many times, "This will be delivered on time, or I'll drop dead trying."

In this project you have no drop-dead time. The only task completion time restraint is you. So let's get a little background on this project.

You are playing the role of husband homeowner. You have a nice home, amazing wife, and two lovely children. For over a year when you return from work you park next to your wife's car in the driveway. You see the garage door and feel the pain of your self-talk.

"I can't believe the garage is so messy. All this money for the house and the garage is full of junk. Will my sister ever come and get her boxes? It must be months that she has stored them here. What a fire hazard. The kids just throw stuff around in there as if they don't care."

IT'S SO MUCH EASIER TO SUGGEST SOLUTIONS WHEN YOU DON'T KNOW TOO MUCH ABOUT THE PROBLEM.

Malcolm Forbes

The facts—
Today's date is: February 1st.
The garage has been a mess for years.

Walking into your home, past the garage door, you feel just a little bit more beaten down: as if the job, the bills, and the commute traffic weren't enough.

As you walk in the door your wife greets you. "You have to do something about the garage, the tree sap is ruining my car, and I got sap on me as I was going into the office this morning. You said that I would be able to park in the garage months ago. (She was being generous; you actually said it many times over the last two years.)

You have a pretty full life already. It is going to take some organization skills to use your time to its fullest and get this garage project done.

While you're changing out of your work clothes you think, "What do I have to do to clean the garage, and how long will each part take?" The reality is that you want the garage back. But, you just haven't moved it up your priority list.

After dinner you go survey the landfill you call a garage. It used to be a spacious two-car garage with a laundry area and a workbench. The laundry area is regurgitating clothing, and the workbench is weighted down with half finished projects mortared together with old magazines, more clothes, and a writhing garden hose. Your stomach feels heavy. There are boxes upon boxes parked where cars should be. Bikes and old bikes, and even older bike parts interwoven with another garden hose, are stacked against one of the garage doors. That door may never be opened again.

To top it all off, cat poop. You can't miss it visually or olfactory, the neighborhood cats are using the place as a litter box.

You're going to have to deal with your sister. Some of the boxes are hers. But at least her boxes are stacked neatly in your parking spot being held down by another garden hose.

Start with breaking down the job into manageable parts. How much time will this really take? Be realistic, not hopeful. If you schedule too much time, great—you're done with time left to do something else. But, if you schedule too little time, you're screwed! You can't make more so you will be stressed.

Parts of the Big Garage Project: Estimated Time

Make project into parts   (0.15 hours)

With clipboard in hand, go out into the garage and survey the project. Break it into areas and responsible party(ies). Also, list any fix-it jobs that need to be done.

Area	Issue /Responsible party(s)	Time estimate
Laundry area	· Piles of laundry: Kid 1 is using the area as extra closet space. · Piles of laundry: Kid 2 is using the area to store dirty clothes. · Messy soap storage area. Shelf broke back during the Jurassic period.	· 30 minutes · 4 hours · See fix-it
Workbench	· Kid 1: art project mess · Kid 2: school project mess · Wife: boxes for donation · Self: the garden sprinkler incident.	· 30 minutes · 30 minutes · 10 minutes · See fix-it
Car one area	· Sister's Boxes	· 1 hour
Car two area	· Self: Workboxes, junk storage, stuff that needs to find a home.	· 4 hours
Garden tool area	· The cool garden tool storage rack is mostly empty. Tools are hopefully intertwined in car one or car two area.	· 1 hour
Fix-it 1: Side door doesn't close correctly.	· The cats are most likely coming in by the side door. It doesn't latch and the wind or the kids leave it ajar.	· 2 hours
Fix-it 2: Fix shelf for soap storage by washer	· Need sturdy shelf for soap storage.	· 2 hours
Fix-it 3: Garden sprinkler	· Locate and protect the $200 worth of sprinkler parts.	· 30 minutes
Fix-it 4: Kill fleas	· The red itchy bumps on your legs are fleabites.	· 15 minutes
	Total:	16 hours 25 minutes

It will take you and your family 16 hours 25 minutes to do a great job on this project. There are only two problems: When do you do it? And, how do you get the others to help?

ORGANIZE THE GARAGE PROJECTS BACKWARDS IN SMALL CHUNKS ON A MONTHLY CALENDAR

You now peruse your monthly calendar and look for 17 free hours to take on a thankless job. You know without even looking, you're not going to find 17 free hours this month. Why this month? The garage has been a mess for months (years), so maybe next month. Stop. Your goal is to clean the garage; you need a drop-dead time.

Without a drop-dead time, you have infinite time. You can easily procrastinate this job far into the future. You need a drop-dead time. You have to give it to yourself as a direct goal.

"I will have the garage spic and span by the end of this month." Now with your drop dead time, you can work backwards, one chunk at a time, through the project.

On the 28th you write: Take photo of both cars in the neat garage.

As you look over the rest of the month you see you have a lot of obligations. Saturdays are full, and many evenings are full. Work hours are full. Your task is to place all the small project chunks on the calendar. And don't forget—if a chunk is too big, break it into smaller chunks.

Not including work and sleep, your calendar looks like:

A POSITIVE ATTITUDE
MAY NOT SOLVE ALL
YOUR PROBLEMS, BUT IT
WILL ANNOY ENOUGH
PEOPLE TO MAKE IT
WORTH THE EFFORT.

Herm Albright

February

Sunday	Monday	Tuesday	Wednesday	Thursday	Friday	Saturday
					Track 3:30-8	1 Soccer game 8-11 am
2	3 Soccer 4-8 PTA meeting 7-9 pm	4	5 Soccer 4-8	6 Soccer 4-8	7 Track 3:30-8	8 Soccer game 8-11 am Mom's Birthday Noon to 5 pm School dance 7-11 pm
9	10 Soccer 4-8	11 Dental 4 pm	12 Soccer 4-8	13 Soccer 4-8	14	15 Soccer game 8-11 am Track all day
16	17 Soccer 4-8	18	19 Soccer 4-8	20 Soccer 4-8	21 Fly out Ralph's Wedding Buffalo.	22 Out of town Ralph's Wedding Buffalo.
23 Out of town Ralph's Wedding Buffalo.	24 Retuning home from Buffalo. 11:30 am Soccer 4-8	25	26 Soccer 4-8	27 Soccer 4-8	28 Take photo of both cars in neat garage.	

Figure 7: Calendar without the garage project

It is now time to organize. However, the garage has fleas. So, before you can assess the project any more, you have to deal with the little beasties.

On today's calendar you write: Buy flea bomb (15 min.) It is getting late, so you decide to run to the overpriced little hardware store to get the flea bomb. It will cost you a few dollars more, but you can set it off before bed tonight. This will allow you to air the garage out first thing in the morning, and start dealing with the project tomorrow afternoon.

After you get the flea bomb; bomb the garage. While the poison is doing its job, you can fill out the rest of the calendar.

The laundry area is the first priority. Sunday looks like this:

All clean clothes removed. Kid 1	(30 min)
All dirty clothes washed. Kid 2	(4 hrs)
Buy parts/fix shelf & fix Door	(4 hrs)
Wash down area	(30 min)

This looks like 9 hours of work, but it is going to be split between three people. All 9 hours can be done Sunday afternoon.

At Sunday breakfast you explain your project to the family. The kids are not impressed. You let them know that your goal is to do the above by 5 pm today.

Not that it would happen at your home, but let's suppose that Kid 2 is all bent out of shape about doing 4 hours of work. You have to use this as a teaching moment.

"The washer and the dryer are doing most of the work," you point out. "Your job is to keep them working efficiently."

Helping your children ask themselves, "What is the next action?", will help them go far in life.

Sunday evening you leave a message for your sister, asking her to come pick up her stuff. You have given similar messages to her over the phone and in person. This time you politely add, "If you haven't picked up your boxes by February the 18th, I will have them delivered to your apartment door."

Without a drop-dead time, your sister is liable to neglect her responsibility. Even with the drop-dead time, you will probably find yourself delivering the boxes to your sister's apartment hallway.

On February 18th you write: Deliver boxes to sister (1.5 Hrs). Note that this is .5 hours longer than you originally planned. The reason is drive time.

For Tuesday the 4th, you write: Get storage boxes on way home from work. You will need them next Sunday.

Sunday the 9th, the troops work together to find the workbench. School projects are finally cleaned up, and the sprinkler parts are found and boxed safely. The garden tool rack is put back into service.

The project is coming along. For Sunday the 16th, you write car area two (4 hrs). This will be a full afternoon of tossing out, re-boxing and storing correctly.

Hopefully, your sister will also come over on the 16th to get her boxes. (Maybe you'll invite her over for dinner on the 16th.) If not, after work on the 18th, you are delivering them to her.

There is a good chance that you and your wife will be parking in your two-car garage by the evening of the 18th. That is ten days before your drop-dead time.

Your calendar now looks like this:

THERE ARE NO SECRETS TO SUCCESS. IT IS THE RESULT OF PREPARATION, HARD WORK, AND LEARNING FROM FAILURE.

Colin Powell

February

Sunday	Monday	Tuesday	Wednesday	Thursday	Friday	Saturday
						1 Soccer game 8-11 am Buy Flea bomb (15 min)
2 All clean clothes removed (30 min) All dirty cloths washed (4 hrs) Buy parts/Fix Shelf & Fix Door (4 hrs)	**3** Soccer 4-8 PTA meeting 7-9 pm	**4** Get storage boxes on way home from work	**5** Soccer 4-8	**6** Soccer 4-8	**7** Track 3:30-8	**8** Soccer game 8-11 am Mom's Birthday Noon to 5 pm School dance 7-11 pm
9 Clean workbench area- Kids (70 m) Organize sprinkler parts. (30 m) Garden tools placed in rack (1 hrs)	**10** Soccer 4-8	**11** Dental 4 pm	**12** Soccer 4-8	**13** Soccer 4-8	**14** Track 3:30-8	**15** Soccer game 8-11 am Track all day
16 Car area two (4 hrs)	**17** Soccer 4-8	**18**	**19** Soccer 4-8	**20** Soccer 4-8	**21** Fly out Ralph's Wedding Buffalo.	**22** Out of town Ralph's Wedding Buffalo.
23 Out of town Ralph's Wedding Buffalo.	**24** Retuning home from Buffalo. 11:30 am Soccer 4-8	**25** Deliver boxes to sister (1.5 hr)	**26** Soccer 4-8	**27** Soccer 4-8	**28** Take photo of both cars in neat garage.	

Figure 8: Calendar with big project

One huge drawback of your plan is that you will have to motivate your children to clean up their mess. In the next section on goal writing, I point out that you can only write goals for yourself. However, this project list is intertwined with parenting. So let me give you a little parenting advice. You can't make your children do anything, but you can motivate them to do lots.

You could simply pick up after the kids, but that will not teach them any responsibility. Also, I'm assuming that the child that is dressing in the garage is breaking some sort of family rule. For a fuller explanation on how to motive your children please see my book, *Basic Parenting 101—The Manual Your Child Should Have Been Born With.*[25]

25- Copitch, Philip. Basic Parenting 101—The Manual Your Child Should Have Been Born With. Hutzpah Press, 2000.

"Oh ... I motivate the kids by waking them up early and telling them that they can't pee until their chores are all done."

"When opportunity came-a-knockin' my Harold just complained about the noise."

5. UNDERSTAND HOW TO WORK YOUR PLAN

Now we roll up our sleeves and set out to make changes in your life. I have read lots of self-help books that get to this part, quickly sum up their ideas, pat you on the head, and wish you well. Not in this workbook. Now we go through the steps to implement the changes in your life that you want to make.

UNDERSTAND WHAT YOU WANT

Ben was an all-American seventeen year old. His father was a doctor, and his mother was a talented party planner. Life was pretty good for Ben's family. They had a nice house, three nice cars, a vacation cottage by a lake, and good friends. Ben's mother and father were worried about Ben.

His mother summed it up this way:

> Ben is a great kid. He is never in trouble, well a little pot and talking back, but he is a good kid. He is respectful and caring. I can't believe I'm even talking to a therapist. Ben is a great kid! But, he is ... how can I say it? I'll just be blunt. Ben's lazy! That's it, lazy to the core. He always has been. He just doesn't care about making something of himself. He would watch TV 'til his eyes fell out if we let him. He is a smart kid, but he just gets by with C's. He refuses to do any homework and he still gets good grades on his tests. The boy is just lazy.

NEVER CONFUSE MOVEMENT WITH ACTION

Ernest Hemingway

When I met with Ben, I asked him what he wanted most in his world. He thought about it a moment, and then his face lit up with enthusiasm.

YOU CAN GET EVERYTHING IN LIFE YOU WANT IF YOU WILL JUST HELP ENOUGH OTHER PEOPLE GET WHAT THEY WANT.

Zig Ziglar

Ben: I want a 1952 Daimler-Benz 300 SL Gull-Wing. It has to be silver with a tan leather interior. It's the best car ever made. It's a work of art and fast as hell.

Dr. Phil: How come?

Ben: It's cool. It's the greatest car on the planet. In its day, it won every major race in the world. It has doors that open like wings!

Dr. Phil: So how come you want the coolest car ever made?

Ben: I want to drive it around and show it off.

Dr. Phil: Show it off?

Ben: That's right, I want to tool on by school and show everyone that I have made it. That I won.

Dr. Phil: Won?

Ben: It probably sounds bad, egotistical and all, but if I had the 300 SL Gull-Wing, I would be the coolest kid in school. Other kids would kill to hang around me.

Dr. Phil: Other kids would be impressed?

Ben: Absolutely. Even if you don't know about cars you would know that this car was the greatest.

GIVE ME A STOCK CLERK WITH A GOAL AND I'LL GIVE YOU A MAN WHO WILL MAKE HISTORY. GIVE ME A MAN WITH NO GOALS AND I'LL GIVE YOU A STOCK CLERK.

J.C. Penny

Dr. Phil: Ben, I don't understand ... do you want the car, or do you want to be the coolest kid in school?

Long pause.

Ben: I never thought about it ... I guess I want to be popular at school.

Dr. Phil: What would being popular at school be like for you?

Ben: I don't get what you're saying here. I don't even like most of the kids at my school.

Dr. Phil: I'm not talking about you liking them, I thought you were talking about them liking you?

Ben: I guess.

Dr. Phil: What would it be like if the kids at school liked you?

Ben: It would be a lot easier. We would say "hi" in the hall. We would do stuff together, I guess.

Dr. Phil: It sounds to me what you really want the most is to have a few friends and more fun in your life.

Ben: That's not wrong, is it?

I'm using my talk with Ben to illustrate that it is hard to really know what we want out of life. I was very impressed with Ben. He showed an amazing amount of insight about himself. This conversation and the realization that comes with it, tends to take six to eight therapy sessions for most young adults. When asked what we want, most of us think of "stuff" that will fix our lives, then later get around to realizing the "stuff" is outside of ourselves. It is nice to have, but it doesn't truly make us feel happy or safe.

You need to truly know yourself. A Chinese proverb goes, "If you don't know where you are going, you are already there." It points out the importance of knowing your destination. If Ben had spent the next twenty or thirty years of his life working towards getting to a life position where he could afford such an expensive car, he probably would not be happy with his purchase. Once he got the car, it is unlikely that his life would change all that dramatically. People would not applaud him when he got out of his snazzy auto. And, he would have the added pressure of wondering if he was liked for himself or for his money.

Ben's life started to change over the next six months. He decided it was important to him that he had friends and that he enjoyed being around people with similar interests. Ben worked on learning how to build friendships. He got choosy about who he befriended. He started to enjoy his days at school for the first time in his life. He decided that he wanted to work with people, and that it might be rewarding to become either a physical therapist or an emergency room doctor. Interestingly enough, when Ben started thinking about his desire to help people, his grades went up. All of a sudden, he was interested in getting into a good college and learning about how he could help people. Once Ben had a goal, he figured out how to reach his goal.

The last time I saw Ben and his mother was at Costco. He was very excited when he told me that he was going to Mexico with a church group to help

THE FIRST STEP TO GETTING THE THINGS YOU WANT OUT OF LIFE IS THIS: DECIDE WHAT YOU WANT.

Ben Stein

IF YOU WANT OTHERS TO BE HAPPY, PRACTICE COMPASSION. IF YOU WANT TO BE HAPPY, PRACTICE COMPASSION.

The Dalai Lama

build a medical clinic. His mother told me, "My Ben is such a good boy. I used to worry about him all the time, I guess I was just being silly." Ben was buying a case of bug repellent for his upcoming trip.

Lots, if not most people, get transfixed on an object that they want. They tell themselves that they will really be happy if they get the perfect house, perfect job, or lots of money. Research shows that Lottery winners are no happier than the general population. If they were happy before their newfound wealth, then they were happy after the windfall. But, if they were unhappy before, they were found to be unhappy millionaires after the money arrived. You cannot buy happiness… you can only rent it. Rented happiness is short-lived and not real.

When it comes to your goals you need to be specific, but not too specific. Sound contradictory? If your goal is to be a professional basketball player, well that sounds great ... unless you are five feet in all directions. As I stated before, you may be a great basketball announcer or a great sports writer or an accomplished athletic trainer, but you are not making it in the National Basketball Association. You are stuck with the limitations the gene pool gave you. If your world orbits around pro B-ball, you need to be there. Finding your niche is what is important.

Shawneva really struggled with the goal list section that follows next. For three weeks I asked her to write down at least ten goals on a piece of paper. She left my office with the best of intentions, returning the next week with platitudes.

"I almost had time to write down my goals on Thursday, but my sister's dog got heat stroke, and I had to drive my sister and Mojo to the pet hospital." She announced as she walked into my office the third week. "I don't know where the time goes, I just don't have time to do your homework." she said.

"My homework? I don't have any homework that I've asked you to do for me. It was your homework. If you don't want to write down your goals, don't. But don't think that your failing has anything to do with me." I explained.

"Failing! I didn't fail. I just didn't do one lousy homework assignment." She sounded angrily defeated.

"Change is an action." I explained. "If you want to accomplish something you have to do something. You have to choose change over whatever is keeping you in your rut. When you were sitting in the vet hospital waiting area you could have written the goal list."

"But, I didn't have the form with me, I'm sorry that I didn't plan better, but I don't keep your home… I mean my homework in the car." Shawneva said.

"You could have done it if you wanted to, on a scrap of paper, or as a text message to yourself, or something." I explained.

Hold this conversation in you mind for a moment. How old do you think Shawneva was?

Shawneva was 45 years old, a mother of two, and owner of four franchise restaurants. I tell you this story of Shawneva because this remarkably organized and skilled woman was unable to write a goal list for herself.

Shawneva's homework assignment was to write a goal list on how to dispose of her husband's belongings as per his Will. Her husband had died six years prior, and Shawneva had not dealt with his estate in all this time.

There are lots of reasons the following assignment may be difficult, each personal to each reader, but you are asking for change in your life. So, let's start that process now.

MY GOAL LIST

On the next page write at least 10 goals you would be proud to accomplish in the next year. Don't be self-conscious; just list your dreams. Your goal list is a commitment to your future self. You can't get this assignment wrong; it's simply a list. But there is one important rule:

> Your goals must be about you. You can't write goals for anyone but yourself.

You only have power over yourself, and at that, only limited power over yourself. You have no power over anyone else. Therefore, you can write, "I want to be in a long term relationship." But you can't

IF YOU WANT TO BE RESPECTED, YOU MUST RESPECT YOURSELF.

Spanish Proverb

AN OUNCE OF ACTION IS WORTH A TON OF THEORY.

Friedrich Engels

write, "I want Sally to love me."

Often the word "want" or "will" is used when writing a goal. Don't get self-conscious about being selfish. We are talking about your wants and desires. You're allowed to be self-absorbed when you are dreaming about the future you.

A few goal examples:

- I will continue walking 4 times per week to maintain my 117 pound weight.
- I want to write a book.
- I want a new job making more money.
- I want to spend three evenings a week with my children.
- I will walk every day.
- I want to join NASA.
- I want to spend July in France.
- I will invite my family to church every week.
- I want to be a millionaire.

Write the goals you would be proud to accomplish in the next year: (at least ten)

1. _____

2. _____

3. _____

4. _____

5. _____

6. _____

7. _____

8. _____

9. _____

10. _____

11. _____

12. _____

13. _____

14. _____

15. _____

16. _____

17. _____

18. _____

19. _____

20. _____

Now, look over your list. Did you follow the rule?

Your goals must be about you. You can't write goals for anyone but yourself.

Examples of correct and incorrect goal writing:

Incorrect: My wife needs to loose weight.

Correct: I will gently talk with my wife about my concerns about her health tonight at dinner.

Incorrect: My boss needs to give me a raise.

Correct: I want to develop a plan for making more money.

Incorrect: I need to stop smoking.

Correct: I want to stop smoking

NEARLY ALL MEN CAN STAND ADVERSITY, BUT IF YOU WANT TO TEST A MAN'S CHARACTER, GIVE HIM POWER.

Abraham Lincoln

Incorrect: Sally should listen to me because I'm her parent.

Correct: I want to be able to communicate with Sally.

Incorrect: I should have invented that.

Correct: I want to be an inventor.

Incorrect: I deserve a @#$% car that works!

Correct: I want a new car!

Incorrect: I'm a fat slob who no one will love.

Correct: I want to weigh less.

Incorrect: I wish people would like me.

Correct: I will plan a lunch date with a friend twice per month.

Incorrect: I wish someone would marry me.

Correct: I will brainstorm and write down what I am looking for in a husband.

I DON'T EXAGGERATE, I JUST REMEMBER BIG.

Juan "Chi-Chi" Rodriguez

Incorrect: The kitchen needs painting.

Correct: I want to paint the kitchen.

Incorrect: Tires are expensive. How can I afford them!

Correct: I will figure out how to afford new tires before the snows come.

SLIGHT EXAGGERATION HELPS

Researchers have found that exaggerating one's present accomplishments leads to better performance. Two studies have found that when college students inflated their grades in conversation, the inflated grades tended to be accurate in future semesters. The grade inflation was about half of a grade. When setting goals, it is usually wise to push yourself.[26,27]

WHAT TO DO WITH YOUR GOAL LIST

It is now time to bring all of our skills together into a cogent force. Here you develop your plan, work it, and accomplish with it. First, some information on how your brain works will help you with your goals.

OVERVIEW OF THE RETICULAR ACTIVATING SYSTEM (RAS) OF THE HUMAN BRAIN

I would like to confess one of my pet peeves. I am bothered when science is misrepresented in popular culture. That's it, I've come clean. I love science. Usually, I just grump to myself. For example, when I'm watching a science fiction movie where a space ship explodes in outer space… why is it so loud? In the vacuum of space, how did the sound waves travel to my ear? There is no sound in a vacuum. Also, what's with the exploding space ship anyway? In most circumstances, wouldn't a spacecraft in space implode? As the artificial atmosphere vented, wouldn't the ship's structure crumble like a beer can on a drunken cowboy's forehead?

Four out of five dentists choose brand X. Nine out of ten doctors recommend Product Y. Who? Under what circumstances are these statistics postulated? That's not the science of statistics, that's finding statistics to help sell your brand X or product Y. (I know a lot of doctors, and from my vantage point, 9 out of 10 doctors think the tenth doctor is a jerk.)

I've had patients concerned that their hands would grow if they applied breast enhancement cream without wearing plastic gloves. (There is no safe cream that will grow breast tissue.) Other patients

THE SELF IS NOT SOMETHING READY-MADE, BUT SOMETHING IN CONTINUOUS FORMATION THROUGH CHOICE OF ACTION.

John Dewey

26- Gramzow, Richard H.; Willard, Greg; Mendes, Wendy Berry "Big tales and cool heads: Academic exaggeration is related to cardiac vagal reactivity." Emotion. 2008 Feb Vol 8(1) 138-144.
27- Richard H. Gramzow and Greg Willard "Exaggerating Current and Past Performance: Motivated Self-Enhancement Versus Reconstructive Memory" Personality and Social Psychology Bulletin, Aug 2006; 32:1114-1125.

have asked if penis enhancement pills work. When I say no, I've been told, "It must, they sell the pills."

When it comes to the common understanding of the human brain, the public is confused. At least once a month someone tells me, "You only use 10 percent of your brain." That's simply wrong. We use all of our brain.

Weekly, a teenager in my office tells me that they are great at multitasking. This same teen tends to be a solid "D" student.

The reality is that the brain cannot multitask.[28,29,30] The brain can only focus on one activity at a time. This may seem contrary to your experience. I once saw a clown juggle while playing a harmonica. You are reading, and breathing, and digesting, and scanning your environment for new sounds. All that is brain multitasking. But, the brain cannot pay attention to two things at one time. For example, do homework and watch TV. The TV may be good background noise for you to study by, but if you know what is going on, on the TV, you are watching TV. If you know what is going on with your homework, you are doing homework. The learning part of your brain is an amazing single task organ.[31 32]

When a person is "multitasking" the brain takes a few hundredths of a second to switch to the next task that it then focuses on. Each refocusing takes a few hundredths of a second. That is very fast, but it has its drawbacks. If the refocusing uses different parts of the brain, then each switch also means that the brain needs to re-access the rules for dealing with each task. The part of your brain that you use for math is different than the part used for feelings. Often, it takes minutes to get back up to speed when switching between intensive tasks. If this isn't inconvenient enough, your memory also gets affected.

One evening, my wife and I were cooking dinner together and having a very pleasant conversation. Our five-year old son ran into the kitchen and interrupted us. He excitedly exclaimed, "On Tuesdays you get mashed potatoes and aardvarks!" He laughed in our general direction and ran off.

We looked at each other and attempted to go back to our pleasant conversation. Neither of us could recall what we had been talking about. We both knew we were enjoying the conversation, but never remembered what we were talking about. Our son's forced refocus-

28- Rubinstein, Joshua S., David E. Meyer, and Jeffrey E. Evans. "Executive Control of Cognitive Processes in Task Switching." Journal of Experimental Psychology: Human Perception and Performance 27.4 (August 2001): 763.
29- Stoet, Gijsbert. "Pay attention!" Psychology Review 13.1 (Sept 2007):19-21.
30- Stoet, G. & Snyder, L.H. (2007). "Extensive practice does not eliminate human switch costs." Cognitive, Affective, & Behavioral Neuroscience, 7(3), 192-197.
31- Duncan, John J., Jr., and Adrian M. Owen. "Common regions of the human frontal lobe recruited by diverse cognitive demands." Trends in Neurosciences 23.10 (Oct 2000):475.
32- Stoet, G. & Snyder, L.H. (2007). "Task-switching in human and non-human primates: Understanding rule encoding and control from behavior to single neurons" In S.A. Bunge and J.D. Wallis (Eds.), pp. 227-254. The Neuroscience of Rule-Guided Behavior. Oxford University Press.

ing of our attention wiped out both of our working (short-term) memories.[33,34,35] (Kids have that effect on their parents.)

If you are switching between known tasks, like washing the dishes, listening to the radio, and watching the kids do their homework in the next room; you can easily switch focus from task to task. But, if you are trying to learn something new, like how to calculate mortgage amortization while listening to the radio, and watching the kids do their homework in the next room, you're setting yourself up to do each poorly. Also, you are likely to become short tempered.

Brain research is in its infancy. But what we do know has been tested and retested.[36] With a little insight into how your brain works, you can substantially increase your goal completion rate.

You and a friend are sitting in your kitchen talking. After a bit, your friend says, "Doesn't your refrigerator bother you?"

"My refrigerator?" you ask.

"Yeah, it's so loud."

"Loud?"

"Yeah, it's driving me nuts."

In all honesty, you hadn't noticed the refrigerator's compressor cycling on. You were used to it.

So, how come you didn't notice the fridge? The answer has to do with a part of your brain called the reticular activating system (RAS).[37] The reticular activating system is comprised of the reticular formation and all of its connections. Working constantly from the core of the brainstem, the reticular activating system plays a major role in keeping you alert. See Figure 9.

33- Tulving, E., & Watkins, M. J. Structure of memory traces. Psychological Review, 1975, 82, 261-275.

34- Bobrow, S. A., & Bower, G. H. Comprehension and recall of sentences. Journal of Experimental Psychology, 1969, 80, 55-61.

35- Craik, F. I. M., & Tulving, E.. (1972). Depth of processing and the retention of words in episodic memory. Journal of Experimental Psychology: General, 104, 268-294.

36- Kuhn, Deanna. "Do Cognitive Changes Accompany Developments in the Adolescent Brain?." Perspectives on Psychological Science 1.1 (March 2006):59(9).

37- The ascending fibers of the reticular formation in the brainstem, defined functionally rather than anatomically according to their control of the level of physiological arousal or activation of the cerebral cortex, essential for wakefulness, attention, and concentration. A Dictionary of Psychology 2001 published by Oxford University Press 2001.

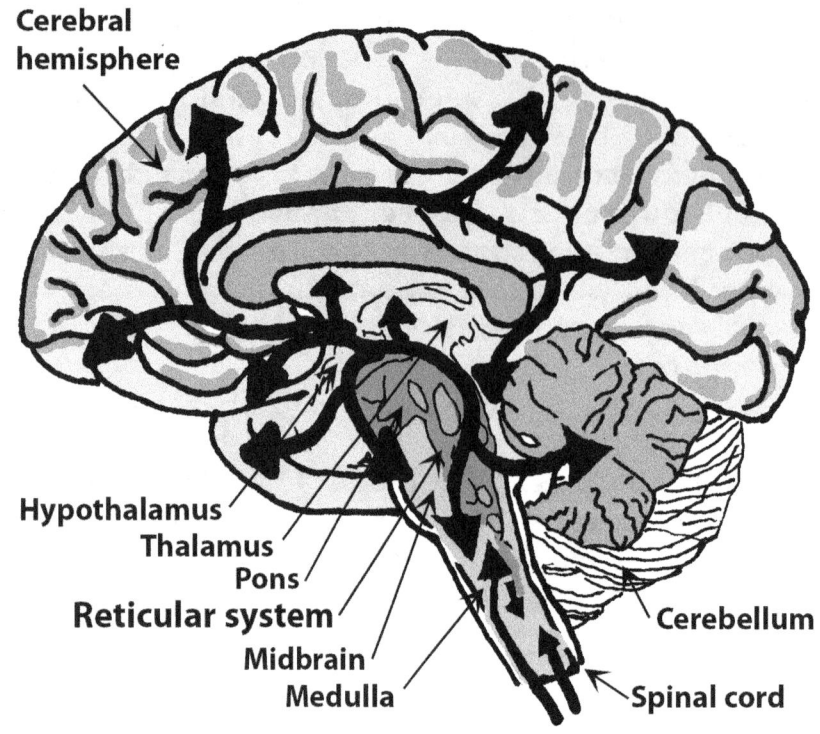

Figure 9: The Reticular Activating System (RAS)

Your reticular activating system allows you to filter external stimulation. According to Dr. Mihaly Csikszentmihalyi, "We filter around 2 million bits of information per second down to 7 plus or minus 2 chunks of information."[38] In milliseconds, your brain factors down a huge amount of information into its usable, essential five to nine bits of information. This occurs, second after second, throughout your life. Without your reticular activating system, all your sensory inputs would have equal value. So, a wildebeest attacking you, and the blue of the sky would be of equal importance to you. Which means you would most likely get stomped to death.

Your reticular activating system keeps track of all of your sensory stimulation (input) and prioritizes it for you, without you consciously having to think about each input.

In the kitchen with your friend, your reticular activating system didn't bother you about the refrigerator compressor, because your RAS didn't perceive that you were in any danger. Your friend's reticular activating system didn't know what to make of your noisy fridge, so it kept forcing your friend's brain to think about it, driving him nuts. Have you ever been distracted to homicidal thoughts because someone was repeatedly clicking a pen? Your reticular activating system kept nudging your thoughts saying, "What's that sound? What's that sound?" The offending pen-clicking-friend's RAS notices the pen click and says, "I know what that is,

---

38- Csikszentmihalyi, Mihaly Flow the Psychology of Optimal Experience. HarperCollins Publisher, March 1990.

I know what that is..." and assigns the noise a very low priority.

Your reticular activating system works for you, standing vigil throughout your life.

The lawyer in my building was telling a story about his new car. "I've only owned it a week, and I'm seeing the exact same color and model all over town." I didn't tell him, but his reticular activating system was pointing out the cars to him. His RAS was saying, "You've been thinking about cars a lot lately, (goal) so I'll point out the kind of cars you seem most interested in."

A mom was concerned that while she was out of town, her husband wouldn't hear the kids at night. She said, "He's such a deep sleeper a formation of howitzers wouldn't wake him." I assured her that dad was up to the challenge, so she reluctantly agreed to let him prove himself.

A few days later, the dad told me, "I can barely sleep. I don't know why, but every little sound wakes me up."

You and I know what's going on, the dad's reticular activating system "knows" that mom is not home and keeps alerting dad to the noises of the kids. When mom returns home, dad's RAS will again lower the nocturnal kid sound vigil to a low priority.

PUTTING THE RETICULAR ACTIVATING SYSTEM TO WORK ON YOUR GOALS

When we make a goal we activate our reticular activating system to search the environment for anything related to our goal. For example, if I'm in an airport, and someone behind me calls out "Bill", my reticular activating system alerts me, and makes me turn around. According to my RAS, "Bill" is close enough to "Phil" in a noisy airport to warrant further investigation. So, there I am, trying to figure out who is waving at me, while playing the last few seconds of my auditory memory tape. "Oh, he said, 'Bill.'" I tell myself. "I'm sure glad I didn't wave."

When you set a goal for yourself, your reticular activating system will point out things that may be of use to you.

If you are house hunting, you notice all the For Sale signs. Interested in a new car? New car ads

> No man can climb the ladder of success without first placing his foot on the bottom rung.
>
> J.C. Penny

seem to be everywhere. Hungry while out and about? Restaurants appear on every street corner. They're always there, but now you notice them.

Russell was an energetic man in his mid-forties. For almost twenty years he had been selling business insurance. He consulted with me because he was concerned about the bickering in his office between employees who had been long-term friends. After meeting with everyone, it turned out the bickering was due to a low level fear that had permeated the office. For years, Russell's insurance business had grown steadily. But, over the last year, business was down just a little. In addition to the decrease in new clients, Russell's business was really a family business. Every employee had a child close to high school graduation. The whole office was very aware that college bills were in their future.

After brainstorming with the group about how to get new clients, it was obvious to them that "they had tried everything." So, to add levity, I asked them if they had used their reticular activating system.

After explaining about the reticular activating system I set up a test. The eight people from the firm and I walked around the neighborhood, each holding a steno pad. As we walked, the goal was to talk about each business we crossed paths with. They were to take notes about what they knew about the business:

- Who owned it?
- Who worked there?

This lead to secondary and tertiary questions such as:

- What business used to be in that location?
- What happened to that business?
- Didn't that business owner used to go to your church, Mary?
- I think his daughter is at Shasta Junior College and is a part time checker at Holiday Market.

After walking around the block, we ended up back at Russell's office. The group was all talkative and happy. After we all sat down, I asked them to go over their notes and make contact with some people they had lost touch with. I emphasized that the goal was to "make contact" not to "sell". "I was thinking of you, and was wondering how you were doing?"

After two weeks, I met with the insurance people again. Each enthusiastically told me about going out to lunch with someone or running into someone else. At the end of the month Russell reported 11 new clients.

"It is kind of magic." Russell said, "Once you suggested we think about people we know, I started seeing them all over town." he said. "I was at the high school basketball game, and must have said five times, 'I was thinking about you the other day as I walked around the block… what are you up to?'"

When you set a goal for yourself, your reticular activating system gets its marching orders. "Inform me of stuff in my environment that may help me get to my goal."

I was teaching a seminar for people who wanted to make mid-life career changes. Most of the attendees were financially comfortable professionals who did not feel emotional fulfillment in their present career.

During a break, an attorney asked me how his reticular activating system could help him find new divorce work. He explained that he was bored to tears doing corporate litigation and he wanted a little action.

I asked him to tell me what his ideal future client looked like. What kind of problem would they be having that his services would be needed? I suggested that he write down his answers and put some time into thinking about "who his client would be."

When we returned from lunch, the attorney shared that the accountant sitting next to him in the seminar was looking for a divorce attorney. He had his first client. As it turned out, he noticed that the accountant was sad after a phone call in the hall. He asked if he was OK and the accountant told him his problems.

Let's test your RAS. You may not have noticed that in the FedEx logo there is a giant arrow.

TALKING MUCH ABOUT ONESELF CAN ALSO BE A MEANS TO CONCEAL ONESELF.

Friedrich Nietzsche

IT'S WONDERFUL WHAT WE CAN DO IF WE'RE ALWAYS DOING.

George Washington

FedEx

There is a white arrow snugly placed between the E and the X. Now that you're aware of it, I suspect that you will notice it for weeks. When a FedEx truck passes by, you will probably want to see the arrow again. The arrow has always been there, but now it is something your RAS "thinks" you want pointed out to you.

Stan told me that after his girlfriend and he broke up, he had to stop listening to the radio. He was amazed that so many songs reminded him of his girlfriend. Stan's reticular activating system was doing its job, making Stan aware of potential danger in his world. I expect country western stations would be the worst. From what I can tell almost every song is about a relationship with either: your girl, your momma or your truck.

WHAT'S THE NEXT ACTION?

As we discussed back in Chapter 3, goals are a lot like eating elephants.

> *"How do you eat an elephant?"* The answer, *"One bite at a time."*
> (If you try to eat an elephant all at once, by hauling it up with a crane and dropping it whole into you mouth. You're one smooched diner. But, if you carve it up you can get it done. If you bite off more than you can chew, you spit it out and cut the piece smaller. Then get back to chewing.)

The seemingly simple task of cleaning off your desk so you can start to get organized, tends to derail people before they really get started. So, let's use this example as a restarting point.

You have a pile, of say, fifty sheets of paper in a semi neat stack before you. You think to yourself, "This is a thankless job, but it needs to be done. But, it will take days! Let's get a cup of coffee instead."

No! Stop! Get back in here! It's only a stack of paper. It's not nuclear waste. The perceived problem with the stack of paper is the sum of its parts. If the stack were last year's completed tax paperwork, the task would be quite simple. Place the stack in an appropriately sized box; mark the box with the content list, and then store the box in a safe place. Finding the box, or a marker, or a location to store it, may be problematic, but still only a few potential problems.

However, with a stack of fifty sheets of paper you could have hundreds or thousands of decisions to make. Some decisions could be fairly easy. The first sheet is a recipe from a food magazine that you want to try. You want to put it with your other recipes at home, but you're at work. So, you hold it in your left hand. The second piece of paper is your Aunt Mabel's phone number. You need this because you need the phone number of Aunt Mabel's daughter, Dora. You have a question for Dora, but don't know how to get in touch with her directly. So now you have a recipe in your left hand and a phone number in your right. Only two sheets in and you have run out of hands. You need a procedure for how to deal with prioritizing this job.

You need to ask yourself "What is the next action?"

Then you judge the answer by time. If it takes less than two minutes, do it now. If more than two minutes, appoint it to be done at a more appropriate time.

Let's re-attack the pile of papers again. Holding the recipe you decide your goal. You want to put the recipe in the cookbook to the left of your toaster oven. The problem is that you are at work, and your cookbook is at home.

"What's the next action?" you ask yourself.

"I'll put it in my wallet and unite it with the cookbook when I get home." But, how well will this work? "What's the next action?" you ask yourself again. "I'll call myself at home and leave the message: 'Put away the recipe that is in your wallet.'" Great that took one minute and 18 seconds.

You pick up the next sheet of paper, Auntie Mabel's phone number. This is not simply a phone number, it is the tip of an iceberg.

Earlier in this chapter, we were looking at incorrect and correct goal setting statements. One of them was:

Incorrect: Tires are expensive. How can I afford them!
Correct: I will figure out how to afford new tires before the snows come.

"I will figure out how to afford new tires before the snows come." This is the tip of the iceberg! The fact that you need new tires is just that, a fact. But how to get them involves a bunch of small decisions, just like Aunt Mabel's phone number. Let me explain.

Your cousin Dora told your sister that she had a $100 off coupon for a set of four tires. Your sister didn't know if Dora was going to use the coupon, but for weeks you have been thinking, "If I can get $100 off the cost of a set of tires, that would be great! But, you don't have your cousin's phone number, and neither did your sister. So, you need to call Aunt Mabel. She will have Dora's phone number. Can this be done in the next two minutes? No. Aunt Mabel is at work until six. You will have to call her tonight.

You appoint Aunt Mabel in your daily planner:

6:45   Call Aunt Mabel (555-1234) Get Dora's Number

6:50   Call Dora _____ about tire coupon

^^^ The space is for the # you get from Aunt Mabel.

You did it! You can now throw away the piece of paper with Aunt Mabel's phone number. Only 48 pieces of paper left in this stack.

I ask myself "What's the next action?" thousands of times each day. I like to be in control of my goals. So what happens if Aunt Mabel says, "I'll be seeing Dora on Saturday, I'll have her call you."

That is very kind of Aunt Mabel, but I am 100 percent responsible for how I deal with my world. If I let Aunt Mabel carry my goal, I'm giving up a lot of control over my destiny. Most people would let Aunt Mabel contact Dora for them. But not me … let me explain.

Mr. Najdorf worked as middle management in a busy Human Resources Department. He complained that he got delayed regularly because someone else in the department didn't complete their task on time. In his last performance review he was marked down for missing deadlines.

"It's not my fault, but I get blamed," he explained. "This past week, a temp worker was late with her research numbers, and I got called on the carpet for it."

I explained about 100 percent self-responsibility and gave him the following example.

I called my insurance agent to ask a question about dental insurance.

"Pen Insurance, Don speaking."

"Hi Don, Phil Copitch here, I know you're busy but I need specific numbers for the dental insurance plan you mailed to me."

"Sure, no problem. I'll have to track them down for you.

"Great, what is the time frame that you need to get back to me?

"Back to you? Ah… how about tomorrow morning?"

"Great, thanks. I'll write on my planner that you will get back to me by noon tomorrow. I appreciate that. Thanks. Bye."

I continued, "I find that when I let the other person tell me what they can do for me, and then I tell them that I am writing it down, they deliver."

Mr. Najdorf was skeptical. "What happens if the insurance man doesn't get back to you tomorrow morning?"

"I wasn't kidding, I wrote it down." I explained. "So at noon I call Don and ask why he didn't do what he said he was going to do. I make sure that I am matter of fact, not accusatory. I am always polite."

I continued, "Most of the time, professionals will do what they say they will do. Especially if they know you wrote it down and are keeping a kind of scorecard. I like to keep in control of my own projects. So for example, if Don had said, 'as soon as I can'. Then I would appoint a time to call him if I hadn't heard from him."

"Sure Don, are you in the office tomorrow?"

"All day."

"Great, I'm writing in my planner to call you at noon tomorrow, if I haven't heard from you. Talk to you then. Bye."

"If Don had said that it would take a week, I would still do the same thing, but appoint it out seven days. I keep control of my project, but I keep others accountable for their parts."

Still skeptical, Mr. Najdorf asked, "I have no real power over my co-workers. I'm the project leader, but I can't fire them. They don't have to listen to me."

"I know," I agreed. "But I still suggest you make them accountable. When we write stuff down it becomes more powerful. After a co-worker agrees to deliver a vital part of your project data, say next Tuesday, write it down."

I suggested that Mr. Najdorf send a confirmation e-mail (note) to them. Such as:

Dear Marie,

    Just a note to thank you for your help with the XYZ report. I am happy to know that you will get me the XYZ data on or before xx/xx/xx at 5 pm. I appreciate your dedication to the completion of this project.

Thanks, Phil

CC: Project XYZ File

Part of getting our goals met is staying on target. We are talking about your goals. You need to manage them.

When you get stuck… ask yourself:
"What is the next action?"

A FEW MORE EXAMPLES OF SETTING PERSONAL GOALS

Incorrect: The kitchen needs painting.

Correct: I want to paint the kitchen.

"What is the next action?"

I will write a list of what I will need to paint the kitchen. I will appoint it in my day planner. I will allot 2 hours to go to the hardware store within the next five days.

Incorrect: I should have invented that.

Correct: I want to be an inventor.

"What is the next action?"

I will write my ideas down. I will keep a small note pad in my back pocket at all times. On Saturday I will go to the library and get a book on how to invent.

Incorrect: Sally should listen to me because I'm her parent.

Correct: I want to be able to communicate with Sally.

"What is the next action?"

I will call Sue and ask for advice on how to talk with Sally.

Incorrect: I need to stop smoking.

Correct: I want to stop smoking

"What is the next action?"

I will smoke three less cigarettes today.

THE COLUMNS LIST TO HELP DEFINE A PATH

We humans want change NOW! And we want a lot of change NOW! So even if it took you twenty years to gain thirty pounds you want it off NOW!

If a relationship took six years to turn to crap you still want it fixed NOW!

If your career was spinning down the toilet for the last fifteen years, you nonetheless want it fixed NOW!

Well it doesn't work that way. Sorry. The process of change counts.

By using the following technique, the Columns of an Outstanding Life, we can keep perspective on how difficult change is.

When you look at Figure 10 you see the basic column. A column is a symbol of a part of your life. For example it could be: work, family, school or love. Each one of these parts itself could have parts. Each part could be its own column. For instance, Family could have your mother, your stepfather, your sister and your cousin.

The column works by asking yourself, "On a scale of 00 (opposite of perfect) to 10 (perfect) how would I rate _____?" You can't get the question wrong. It is your opinion.

IF YOU WANT TO MAKE PEACE, YOU DON'T TALK TO YOUR FRIENDS. YOU TALK TO YOUR ENEMIES.

Moshe Dayan

"On a scale of 00
(opposite of perfect)
to 10 (perfect)
how would I rate
_____?"

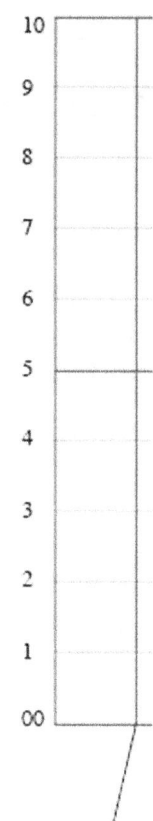

Figure 10: Columns List

So, for this example let's say you are feeling angry with your sister, Sissy. And you ask yourself the question, "On a scale of 00 to 10, how would I rate my relationship with Sissy?"

You rate it as 5.5. What does a 5.5 mean? Only you really know. Your 5.5 rating is personal to you. It's not a 6.0 but it is better than a 5.0.

Figure 11 shows your column rating of 5.5.

Now this is where people tend to fight me. The next question is: "What do you have to do to get it from 5.5 to 6?" At this point I hear, "6 - I want a 9 or a 10!"

I understand; we all want perfect, but process counts. What do you need to do to get it to a 6?

"Me, why do I need to get it to a 6? She is the one who regularly causes difficulties. How come I have to fix her problems?"

This tends to be the trouble. We only have control over ourselves. We can only write goals for ourselves. So, you need to think of what you can do to get from a 5.5 to a 6 in your relationship with Sissy.

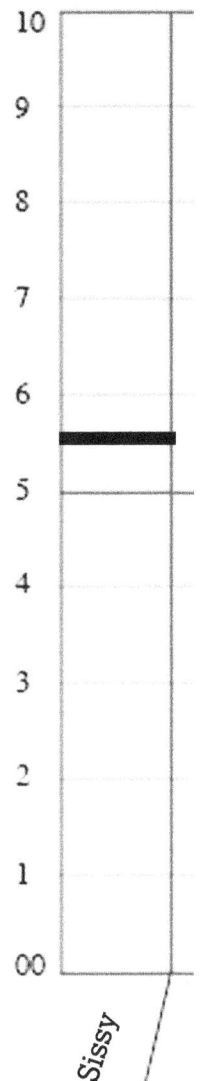

"ON A SCALE OF 00 (OPPOSITE OF PERFECT) TO 10 (PERFECT) HOW WOULD I RATE _____?"

Sissy

Figure 11: Relationship with Sissy

Gary was very upset about not being invited to a monthly family get together at Sissy's home. After Gary spent ten minutes explaining how all that was wrong with the world was Sissy's fault, I asked him to rate his present relationship with his sister.

Gary: "We used to be an 8. But now, I guess a 5.5"

Dr. Phil: "Guess?"

Gary: "Yeah. A 5.5."

Dr. Phil: "What do you have to do to get it from 5.5 to 6?"

Gary: "I could stop hounding her about her smoking."

Dr. Phil: "Would that get you to a 6?"

Gary: "At least a 6. I've really been on her about her smoking."

A week later Gary and I talked again.

Dr. Phil: "How would you rate your relationship with Sissy this week?"

Gary: "A 7."

Dr. Phil: "Are you ok with a 7?"

Gary: "No."

Dr. Phil: "What do you have to do to get it from 7 to 7.5?"

Gary: "I need to pay her husband back the money I borrowed."

Dr. Phil: "Borrowed?"

Gary: "I had car problems and I borrowed the money until my next paycheck. I was behind on other bills and just kind of avoided them for a week. This really upset Sissy."

Dr. Phil: "Can you pay them back?"

Gary: "I'll see them on Sunday and pay them back."

Dr. Phil: "Not that it is any of my business, but what was it all about—the smoking argument.

Gary: Sissy was hinting around that I needed to pay back the loan, and I told her that she wasted money on cigarettes. This really upset her. She is trying to stop smoking, but it is hard.

When we use the column technique honestly with ourselves, we often find the way to meet our goals. As a reminder, if we let the Thought Mines get in our way we will be sabotaging our own goals.

THE SOLUTION IS TO GRADUALLY BECOME FREE OF SOCIETAL REWARDS AND LEARN HOW TO SUBSTITUTE FOR THEM REWARDS THAT ARE UNDER ONE'S OWN POWERS. THIS IS NOT TO SAY THAT WE SHOULD ABANDON EVERY GOAL ENDORSED BY SOCIETY; RATHER, IT MEANS THAT, IN ADDITION TO OR INSTEAD OF THE GOALS OTHERS USE TO BRIBE US WITH, WE DEVELOP A SET OF OUR OWN.

Mihaly Csikszentmihalyi
Flow: The Psychology of Optimal Experience

LET'S LOOK AT A BUSINESS EXAMPLE.

Del was procrastinating a business decision concerning a $250,000 fall advertising promotion. He broke the parts into six columns. Each column was a small part of his larger problem. For each column he asked himself the question, "On a scale of 00 to 10 how would I rate _____?"

He ended up with four 8's and two 2's. He went back to his ad team and reworked the 2's to 2.5. Then to 3. Then to 4. After two weeks of agony, the team got to 6 for each of the last two columns. That gave them four 8's and two 6's. With their well thought out, but not perfect plan, they launched their promotion.

About a month into the promotion, I met with Del and asked him about his fall ad campaign.

"It is hard for me to pull the trigger on a quarter of a million dollar campaign. By working the parts, I was able to keep my anxiety under control. It helps me sleep at night."

ACCOUNTABILITY AND THE COLUMNS LIST

Up to this point, I have only shown you part of the columns list. Figures 12 and 13 are the whole thing. A full-page version for you to copy is available at the back of this workbook. One major problem about making personal change is that it tends to be private. If your goal is to lose some weight and you say to yourself, "I am not eating fast food for the rest of this month!" that is all well and good, but it has no accountability. Come lunchtime during your busy day, you pop into Mickie D's because you're busy and you are not beholden to anyone but yourself. (You can easily give yourself permission to eat fast food because of the justifications that are running through your head.) But, what if you told your girlfriend that you were not eating fast food for the rest of this month, and had gone as far as asking if you could check in with her at the end of the day simply to tell her if you kept to your convictions. Your likelihood of choosing fast food goes down if you have accountability outside of yourself. The person you make yourself answerable to has no power over you. You are simply making yourself accountable to them. In this situation,

WHEN YOU ARE NOT PHYSICALLY STARVING, YOU HAVE THE LUXURY TO REALIZE PSYCHIC AND EMOTIONAL STARVATION.

Cherrie Moraga

your girlfriend doesn't get to chastise, punish, guilt or belittle you. She gets to know, because she agreed to help you be accountable. If you kept your goal, that is it.

The act of making yourself accountable to someone will vastly increase your success rate.

The Accountability Section is where you write down your accountability agreement. The first square is for you to indicate what column you are working on.

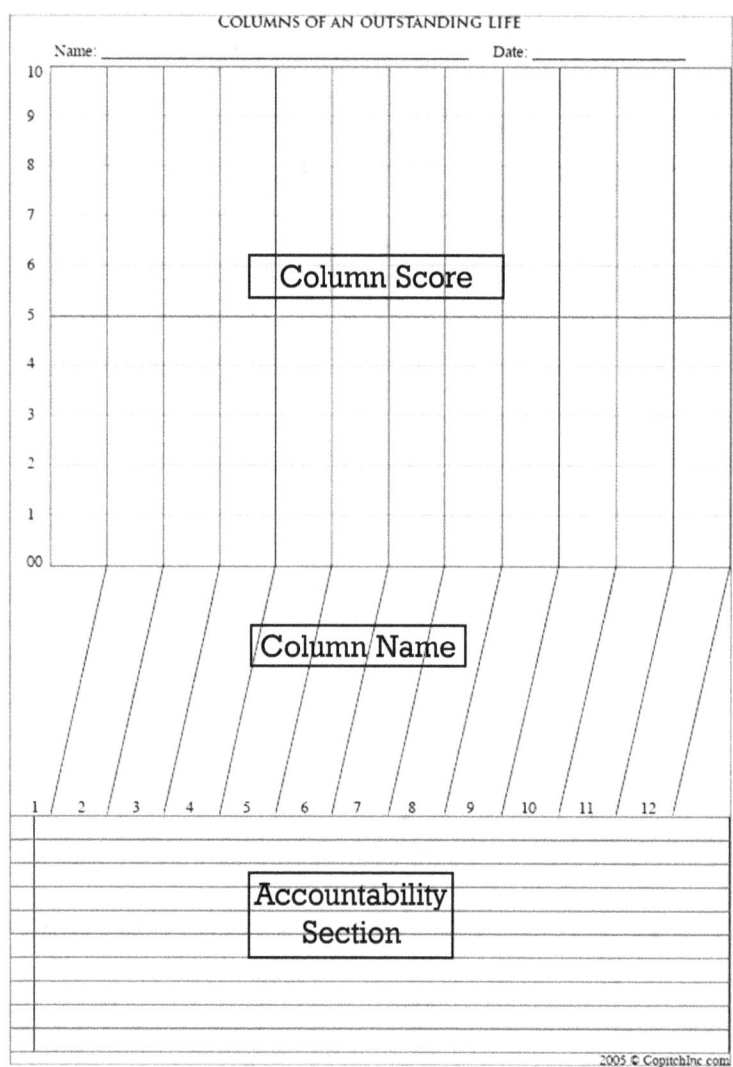

Figure 12: Parts of the Column List

Figure 13 is an example of a completed Columns List. It is not earth shattering. The power is in its simplicity.

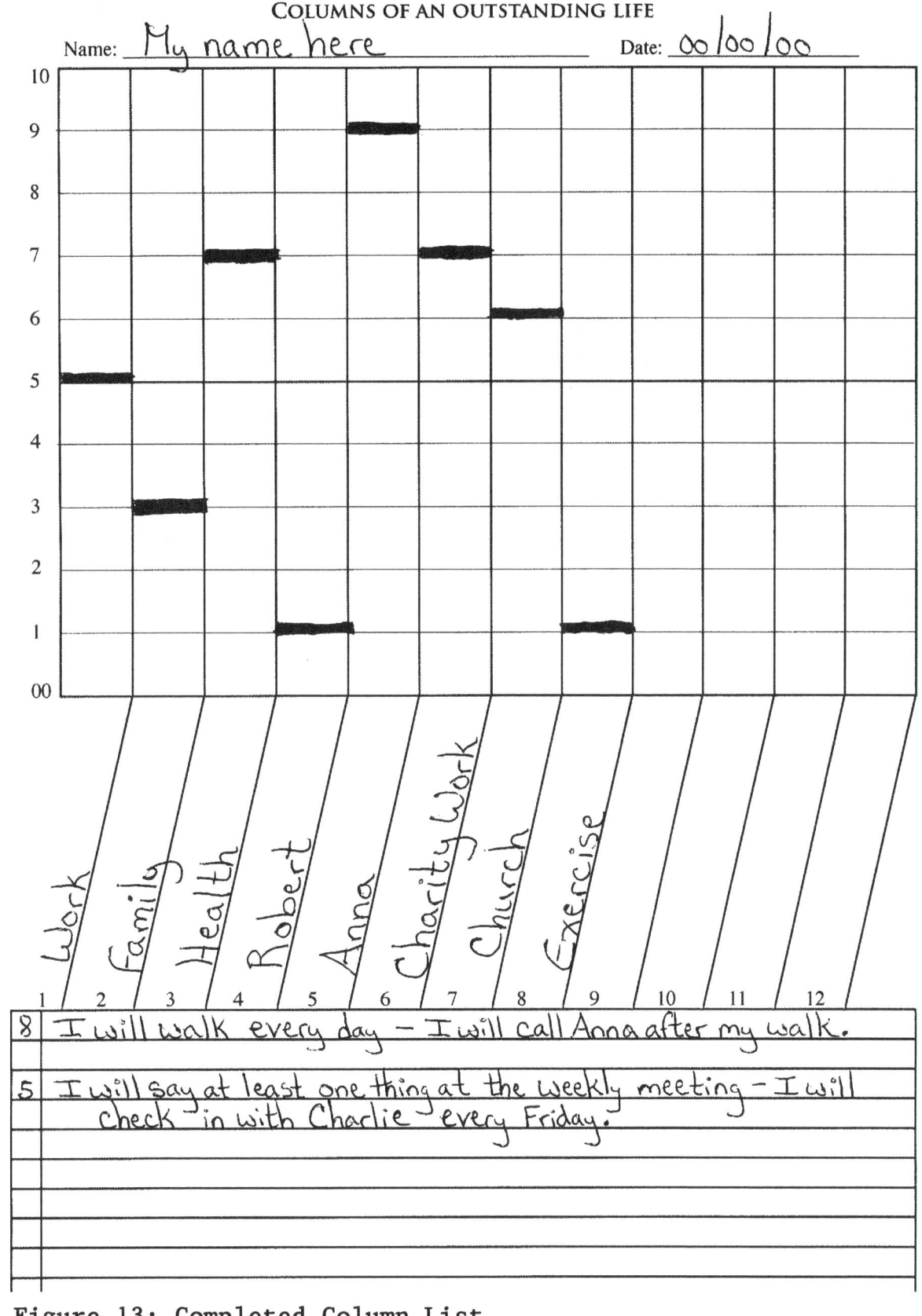

Figure 13: Completed Column List

I advise you to keep past forms so you can check your progress over time. One of my patients called it her "Goals Diary."

Additional Column Lists can be found at the back of this workbook.

ACCOUNTABILITY SECTION

Hal and Bobbie came to me for advice. As it turned out, Bobbie was very concerned about Hal's diabetes, and Hal was positive that Bobbie was overreacting. For three weeks, Bobbie had been scouring the Internet for information on diabetes. She had printed out hundreds of articles and left them scattered all over the house, hoping that Hal would read them. She had purchased three new diabetic cookbooks and regularly asked Hal to pick out a recipe that she would happily make for him.

"I have become a project for her, she is driving me nuts." Hal said.

Defensively Bobbie explained, "I'm just trying to help. Diabetes is very dangerous. You can go blind or die prematurely."

After I explained that we cannot write goals for anyone but ourselves, Bobbie confessed. "That makes sense, but I'm so worried."

"I'm a little worried too." Hal said. "But as my daddy used to say, 'You can't cash another man's paycheck.'"

After explaining the columns list, Hal gave himself a rating of 3 on "Health". To go from 3 to 3.5 Hal decided to switch from sugar to Splenda in his morning coffee.

To help himself with his goal achievement, Hal asked Bobbie:

"Now, come morning when I sit down at the Pancake House for my coffee, I'll use that yellow stuff. When I call you, I'll tell ya that I did it and you don't get all happy or nothing."

Bobbie was happy to comply with her support role. As it turned out, morning coffee was one of her biggest concerns. For twenty-five years, Hal and the other farmers met for morning coffee. Hal would fill his cup halfway with sugar, and then the waitress would add coffee. Hal never stirred his coffee. The waitress would keep toping off Hal's cup. Over the next half hour lots of coffee and sugar went into Hal. Hal called Bobbie every morning from the Pancake House during Bobbie's break at school, where she worked as a cook.

A few weeks later, Hal reported his health rating to be a 5. Without me asking, he told me how he planned to go from a 5 to a 5.5.

"Three days a week, I'm going to meet Bobbie at school. They have this exercise walk and we're going to walk it."

Bobbie added, "I need to watch my weight, and this we can do together."

HOW OTHERS HAVE MADE PERSONAL CHANGES

We are almost at the end of this workbook. I hope you find your own particular concerns addressed in different parts of it. By picking and choosing the sections that apply to you personally, this workbook becomes useful to you. By investigating these parts of yourself you will gain mastery over your life. Over the next few pages I want you to see how others have integrated this information into amazing life changes.

Walter, age 45: Married with two teen girls.

"Once I realized that I was writing goals for my daughters my life got better. I used to yell a lot but nothing changed. My frustrations led me to thoughts of divorce and abandonment.

"I watched my self-talk and found that I was constantly belittling my family. I only said the nasty thoughts when I was really angry, but I thought them all the time.

"I used the Thought Mine - Mind Reading to make myself crazy. This led to lots of misunderstanding and often put me on the defensive. By dealing with my Time Bandits I have found lots of time to be with my girls. I have put work in its place, and I don't use work as an excuse anymore."

Dr. Nancy, age 52: Married with two grown children.

Dr. Nancy and I were talking over lunch at a seminar.

"I always thought you were weirdly calm," Dr. Nancy confessed. "I know you are excited about life, but you are calm. I've seen you testify in court, and you were calm. I've seen you deal with truly

THERE ARE TWO MAIN STRATEGIES WE CAN ADOPT TO IMPROVE THE QUALITY OF LIFE. THE FIRST IS TO TRY MAKING EXTERNAL CONDITIONS MATCH OUR GOALS. THE SECOND IS TO CHANGE HOW WE EXPERIENCE EXTERNAL CONDITIONS TO MAKE THEM FIT OUR GOALS BETTER.

Mihaly Csikszentmihalyi
Flow: The
Psychology
of Optimal
Experience

THE ILLITERATE OF THE 21ST CENTURY WILL NOT BE THOSE WHO CANNOT READ AND WRITE, BUT THOSE WHO CANNOT LEARN, UNLEARN, AND RELEARN.

Alvin Toffler

horrible clinical cases, and you were calm. I have always been secretly amazed.

"It wasn't until I read your book that I understood that your calmness could be learned. And, that I could learn it too. When I looked at my Black and White Thinking I started to develop calmness. When I monitored my self-talk I realized that I was always a little afraid, even though I have nothing to be afraid of.

"I find that by only attempting to change a little at a time, I get change. I used to be so frustrated. I am constantly asking myself 'What's the next action?' which is so empowering. I used to say, 'What do I have to do now!' and wished for any distraction."

"Thanks," I said, "Are you going to buy me lunch?"

Dr. Nancy smiled, "Sure, but only because it's part of the seminar."

Mary, age 67: Widowed 10 years, no children.

"When I realized that I can act out an emotion, but I am not an emotion, my life started to get better. It was hard at first to monitor my own body language, so I started stepping in front of a full-length mirror to see my own feelings. If my shoulders were down and my face was sad, I noticed I was stuck in self-pitying self-talk. I was pushing people away because they thought I was a grumpy old lady. But I'm not! I'm nice and I'm funny, but after Bernie died, I forgot to act nice and fun.

"My self-talk was holding me back. I used to say a hundred times a day, 'I can't do that because I'm too fat.' When I learned about (the Thought Mine) Size Problem I understood I was holding myself back. I now get out. I have a life and I am really enjoying volunteering at the thrift store. I have met loads of nice people at the charity. I even play bunko with some ladies from there. I'm not very good, so I always lose. But, I do laugh a lot as I lose."

Glen, 27: College student.

"I found the Thought Mines section hard to understand. On my third read through, I understood why. I tend to use Negative Labeling to blame others and push people away. When I read the Thought Mines section I kept seeing my family. A lot jumped out at me. I used my self-talk to destroy everyone around me. When I started to look at my frameworks I realized I was really hurting myself.

"The section on Forgiveness allowed me to move on and leave my anger in the past.

"My goals are solid grades. I now have a planner and I keep track of my time. My study habits really improved as I got organized. I like that I am 100% responsible for my life.

"I have noticed that I am changing friends. I don't want to be held back any more.

Norman 33: Business owner and divorced father of one.

"I am a nice guy, but I seem to get stepped on all the time. Over the last two years I have been building my business and taking care of my daughter. It has been hard because I have to work around my daughter's school schedule.

"After my wife got arrested for methamphetamine sales, I was devastated. I thought that rehab was going to work. I blamed myself for not knowing how involved with drugs she really was.

"My self-esteem was lower than low. When I learned that I could rebuild my self-esteem like a bird builds a nest, I felt hope. I want my daughter to have it way better than her mom or me. I make sure that she can build her self-esteem strong by giving her good building materials to work with.

"I used Fortune Telling a lot and found that I misread people all the time. By keeping my Fortune Telling in check and staying focused on my work, we are doing great. I used to waste a lot of time worrying, time that I don't have. I have become very aware of Time Bandits.

"My pastor allows me to use him as my accountability go-to guy. Knowing that I can tell him my little wins really helps. It keeps me focused on building my business. I used to think that I had to hit a home run to solve a problem. But now I think to myself, 'What's the next action?' I haven't had the weight of an elephant sitting on my chest in a long time."

Gretta, age 42: Newly married.

"I have always felt that I was blessed. I have always had interesting work and great friends. But deep inside I had a need to please everybody.

"I was really surprised when I found out that I had severe hypertension. My doctor said I was stressed out. This didn't make sense to me. I thought everyone was stressed out. I thought that stressed out was normal.

"My self-talk was constantly racing. You see that is what happens if you are a people pleaser. I over analyzed every conversation. I lost sleep worrying about nonsense.

"Now I have perspective. I exercise and have taken control over my time. When I learned about 86,500 seconds I thought, 'There must be time for a man in all those seconds.' And I was right. I found him about a year ago at the gym and I'm holding onto him tight.

"Once I decided what I really wanted in life was all I had plus a husband, I organized a plan. I have always been good at setting business goals. I just never thought of setting personal goals. I decided what I wanted, and I made time for me so I could find him. What I find most interesting is that I now only work 45 hours a week, and still get everything done."

Jeremy Age 23: Single.

"When I first read over the Thought Mines I figured I was really messed up. Almost every one seemed like me. I kept thinking to myself that everybody knows how to get their needs met but me.

"The section on purifying my beliefs helped me a lot. I realized that I was asking snide questions and then beating myself up with my self-talk sarcastic answers. I'd ask, 'How come I'm not happy?' and answered, 'Because I'm a loser.' 'Why don't I exercise? Because I'm a fat pig.' I'd been doing it since I was a kid, so I was used to it, I guess.

"I never thought I could think differently. But when I learned, 'How can I do it differently?' I started asking myself better questions. Not snide questions, but better, helpful questions. Now I ask, 'What can I do to lose weight?' and I answer, 'Go for a walk.' I can ask, 'How can I feel happy?' and I answer, 'Life rewards action.' So I act happy until my brain catches up with my body.

"Knowing that 'action cures fear' has helped me try new things. I took a pottery class last semester. I was terrible at it, but I had so much fun."

To follow you will find five Columns Lists. This is to get you started. In the Forms section at the end of this workbook is a master for you to use to make copies of.

Action cures fear

Change starts now ... what is your next action?

COLUMNS OF AN OUTSTANDING LIFE

Name: _____   Date: _____

10											
9											
8											
7											
6											
5											
4											
3											
2											
1											
00											

1   2   3   4   5   6   7   8   9   10   11   12

COLUMNS OF AN OUTSTANDING LIFE

Name: _____   Date: _____

10												
9												
8												
7												
6												
5												
4												
3												
2												
1												
00												

1   2   3   4   5   6   7   8   9   10   11   12

COLUMNS OF AN OUTSTANDING LIFE

Name: _____   Date: _____

10											
9											
8											
7											
6											
5											
4											
3											
2											
1											
00											

1	2	3	4	5	6	7	8	9	10	11	12

COLUMNS OF AN OUTSTANDING LIFE

Name: _____   Date: _____

10												
9												
8												
7												
6												
5												
4												
3												
2												
1												
00												

1 2 3 4 5 6 7 8 9 10 11 12

COLUMNS OF AN OUTSTANDING LIFE

Name: _____ Date: _____

10 |||||||||||||
9 |||||||||||||
8 |||||||||||||
7 |||||||||||||
6 |||||||||||||
5 |||||||||||||
4 |||||||||||||
3 |||||||||||||
2 |||||||||||||
1 |||||||||||||
00 |||||||||||||

1   2   3   4   5   6   7   8   9   10   11   12

6. IN CONCLUSION: BE CREATIVE... GO DO WELL!

Personally, I hate getting to the end of a good book when my relationship with the characters must come to an end. The end of the book means I won't get to know anything more about the characters I have spent time learning to love or hate.

This workbook is not that way. The end of this workbook is the beginning of your next chapter in life. In fact, the majority of your life is probably still ahead. I wish you all the very best.

Over the course of this workbook, I have covered how you can take control of your life. By being aware of your self-talk and emotional frameworks, you can find calm. By understanding goal setting and controlling time, you can accomplish. And by putting it all together, you can be outstanding. I hope you truly enjoy your gift of life.

Please indulge me for one last story. I wrote it many years ago for another book , but I think it fitting to retell it here:

> Years ago my wife, Geri, suggested that we take the family to a favorite camping area from her youth. She painted a beautiful picture of secluded campgrounds dotting a reflecting lake in the Adirondack Mountains of upstate New York. She talked about how we could rent canoes and paddle to the silent woods. She spoke of her hope that, if we were lucky, we could get the campground on the small island in the middle of the picture postcard lake.
>
> Over the next few weeks we made plans to fly to the east coast and meet up with other family members to camp at Forked Lake. Our summer vacation plans came together.
>
> As we drove to Forked Lake from Grandmother's house, the skies were gray and threatening. The weather had been cold and rainy for many days. We talked about how we were going to have to make the best of our camping trip, no matter the weather. When we got to the state campground entrance the cloud cover opened and patches of bright blue snuck through. The first

MANY PEOPLE THINK THAT IF THEY WERE ONLY IN SOME OTHER PLACE, OR HAD SOME OTHER JOB, THEY WOULD BE HAPPY. WELL, THAT IS DOUBTFUL. SO GET AS MUCH HAPPINESS OUT OF WHAT YOU ARE DOING AS YOU CAN AND DON'T PUT OFF BEING HAPPY UNTIL SOME FUTURE DATE.

Dale Carnegie

LET US, THEN BE UP AND DOING,

WITH A HEART FOR ANY FATE;

STILL ACHIEVING, STILL PURSUING,

LEARN TO LABOUR AND TO WAIT.

Henry Wadsworth Longfellow

LOOK NOT MOURNFULLY INTO THE PAST. IT COMES NOT BACK AGAIN. WISELY IMPROVE THE PRESENT. IT IS THINE. GO FORTH TO MEET THE SHADOWY FUTURE, WITHOUT FEAR.

Henry Wadsworth Longfellow

thing we did was check on the availability of the island campsite. The ranger was blunt, "It's been raining for near two weeks, take your pick." We rented the island campsite and were afloat in the canoes in record time.

The lake was choppy and the wind cold. The sun threatened to burst into full light, but for now it was just hope. Ethan and I started off in our canoe. The first ten minutes were exciting as I steered the bow of the canoe towards the island. In short order, the canoe trip to the small island became work. Ethan quickly lost his enthusiasm for the sea. He was in serious need of a nap. The wind was cold and damp. The camping equipment laded the boat.

The mountain storm had washed a lot of debris into the lake. Steering around the floating branches and entertaining Ethan became cumbersome. After twenty minutes of paddling we met up with a cross flow of water. The wind was bitterly moist and cold. Ethan was complaining. To my surprise, the island seemed very far away.

Between the wind and drizzle, cross current, and debris, the canoe trip took over an hour. A very long hour. Setting up camp was a chore and getting everyone warm was work. But, it all worked out. We spent a magical sunny week on "our" private island.

A few months later I was talking with a couple about their two-week summer vacation. It was horrible. Many things went wrong. It tried their relationship to the breaking point. By the end of the fourth day they returned home, completely upset with each other, and filed for divorce. On the advice of their friends they sought marriage counseling.

I told them the story of Forked Lake. Then continued:

I have thought about that canoe trip often. After the weather turned nice, we canoed the same route many times. It was a leisurely twenty-minute trip.

I found myself thinking about how the first canoe trip was so hard. As it happened I felt frustrated. I constantly had to redirect my canoe. Something seemed to constantly pull me away from my target.

I think of my marriage and my family in a similar way. I know where I want to be say, in fifty years. But, something is constantly pulling or pushing me away from that goal. On the rainy canoe trip my goal was the island. When something misdirected me, I had to navigate around it. I found a way to deal with it, as best I could, and then pointed my canoe back at my target.

It seems to me, that in life we are constantly blown off course and have to deal with the problem and then get ourselves back on target.

THE BEST WAY TO PREDICT THE FUTURE IS TO INVENT IT.

Alan Kay

So, in closing, I hope that you hear that the process of raising yourself counts. The end result is your target island, your goal, and your dreams. But, the day-to-day process of getting to your island is the hard built foundation that is your life.

Allow yourself the peace of mind to know that you will be blown off course. And, the serenity that comes from knowing that you will deal with the problem and redirect yourself toward your island. The process counts.

I LOOK TO THE FUTURE BECAUSE THAT'S WHERE I'M GOING TO SPEND THE REST OF MY LIFE.

George Burns

Thank you for taking your time to read my workbook. I hope you have found it helpful.

Thank you for encouraging my behavior,

'I WISH LIFE WAS NOT SO SHORT,' HE THOUGHT. 'LANGUAGES TAKE SUCH A TIME, AND SO DO ALL THE THINGS ONE WANTS TO KNOW ABOUT.'

J. R. R. Tolkien

(PC)

Philip Copitch, Ph.D.
2008

7. FORMS

The following forms are here for you to use as masters. Use them to make clean copies.

"If my boyfriend is all that bad, why is he doing 500 hours of community service?"

COLUMNS OF AN OUTSTANDING LIFE

Name: _____   Date: _____

| 10 |
| 9 |
| 8 |
| 7 |
| 6 |
| 5 |
| 4 |
| 3 |
| 2 |
| 1 |
| 00 |

1 2 3 4 5 6 7 8 9 10 11 12

Month:

Year:

Sunday	Monday	Tuesday	Wednesday	Thursday	Friday	Saturday

Do List

Index

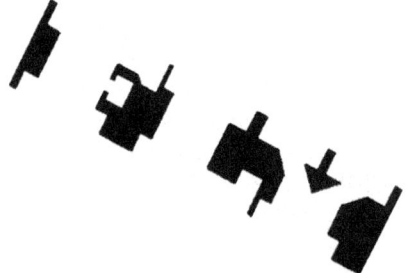